Geoffrey Bucknall's Book of

FLY~FISHING

By the same author:

Geoffrey Bucknall's Book of
FLY-FISHING

Illustrations by Noel Messenger

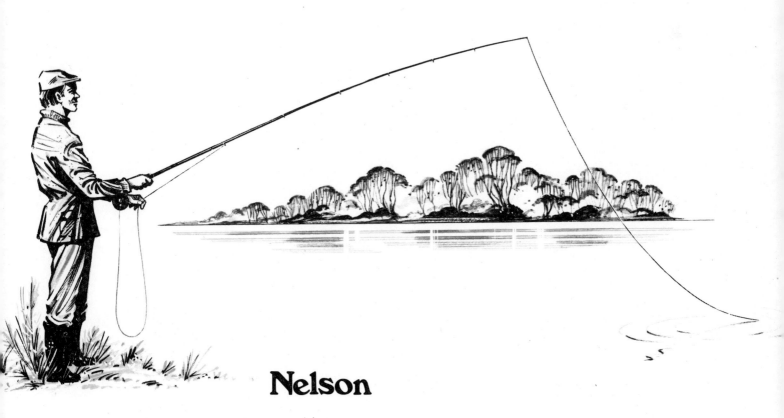

Nelson

Thomas Nelson and Sons Ltd
36 Park Street London W1Y 4DE
PO Box 18123 Nairobi Kenya

Thomas Nelson (Australia) Ltd
597 Little Collins Street Melbourne 3000

Thomas Nelson and Sons (Canada) Ltd
81 Curlew Drive Don Mills Ontario

Thomas Nelson (Nigeria) Ltd
PO Box 336 Apapa Lagos

First published in Great Britain by
Thomas Nelson and Sons Ltd

Copyright © 1974 Geoffrey Bucknall

Illustrations by Noel Messenger,
copyright © Thomas Nelson and Sons Ltd

ISBN 0 17 149068 1

Printed in Great Britain by R. J. Acford

Contents

Half-tone Illustrations

ACKNOWLEDGEMENTS

I wish to acknowledge the invaluable help of W. J. Howes who provided most of the photographs used in this book, and also that of Brian Harding who took the photographs for the bulk of the fly-casting sequences. Other acknowledgements are due to R. Ward and John Palmeri for photographs, and to James Gilmour with whom I discussed distance casting on still water so many years ago.   G.B.

1 Fly Casting

Why is fly casting so completely different from other casting methods, as in sea or coarse fishing? The answer is in the virtual absence of a weight to cast. The sea angler has to hurl out four or six ounces of lead, while the float fisherman has the weight of his terminal tackle, his float and split shot. The weight of the artificial fly is minute, and from this fact stems an entirely different concept in tackle and method.

It would oversimplify matters to state that the casting weight is built into the line, for although this is true, the weight of a fly line is not on the end of the tackle. It increases progressively the longer line there is to be cast. Therefore the rod has to act as a spring, in much the same way as the old coachman's whip. If the rod is the spring, the weight of line is its load, while the arm and wrist act both as provider of the initial energy and as an anchor against which the spring must flex.

The chief problem that a sea or coarse fisherman has to overcome is the built-in memory of trying to swing out a terminal weight which isn't there. He is forever driving the line forward without first having wound up the spring. This is why we describe the casting act as two separate movements, the 'back cast' and the 'forward-cast'.

The human brain works in a strange way when learning those simple actions requiring a series of co-ordinated movements, whether it be the golf swing, cricket stroke or fly cast. When it doesn't work out, we break it down into its component parts in our minds, analyse them to discover the supposed error, then work on correcting this mistake. This is the worst approach of all, for the fly cast must be viewed positively. The learner must concentrate on 'putting it together', rather than breaking it down. This bad mental approach is caused by the unavoidable description of the cast as movements in sequence, which is emphasised by series of illustrations, freezing the cast at a particular moment in time.

The right approach is to study these pictures and stages of casting while trying to visualise them as a continuous action with a definite result. Only one thing more need be said about this now: fly casting is easy, but you may cause yourself trouble and confusion by trying to make yourself into a good caster by eliminating errors. Learn how to do it correctly from the start rather than try to arrive at a good cast by avoiding every possible departure from the routines described. I must, of course, describe the cast in sequence, and point out common errors. When you practise, though, think positively. 'What must I do right?' Not 'What am I doing wrong?'

Simple, Overhead Fly Cast

The modern way of teaching any sport is to put the tools into your hand immediately, so that you get the feel of them. Then you learn the basic movements, and only after this do you move on to the mechanical theory of the tool itself. I assume now that you have the fly rod, correctly loaded with line, and a small length of nylon attached to the end of the line to prevent it cracking. It's better if you are by a pool, but this cast can also be mastered on grass, harder surfaces being unkind to costly fly lines. Water makes casting easier, as we shall see, but there's nothing wrong with back garden fly casting!

All you need to know is that you have a fly rod in your hand, length about 8 ft. 10 in to 9 ft. for general-purpose fishing. The 3½-in. reel will hold a size 6 double-taper fly line, suitably backed with braided line.

The Grip: How to Hold the Rod

The correct way to grip the rod is shown in the illustration. The fingers are curled round the butt with the thumb on top, holding the rod towards the end of the cork handle. The wrist lies along the rod butt above the reel. This grip should be neither too fierce nor too lax, and has been described as the pressure you would need to hold a kitten firmly without hurting it or allowing it to escape. The ball of the thumb rests firmly on the cork and plays the most important part of the cast.

The right hand thus holds the rod. The first thing to learn is to lay out a nice, straight twelve yards of line. This is best done without the left hand coming into play, but as the line has to be kept tight throughout the cast, the

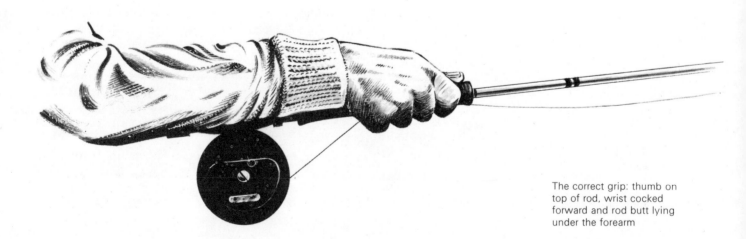

The correct grip: thumb on top of rod, wrist cocked forward and rod butt lying under the forearm

forefinger of the right hand pinches the line against the underside of the butt, as it comes off the reel.

The Casting Movements

Keep it firmly in your mind that the rod is a spring, the energy of which is to propel the line forward. The first important action is to wind up the spring against its anchor, the wrist. This is done by throwing the line smartly to the rear. If you imagine yourself as the hub of a clock, the steam is put into the rod at approximately 10.30. When the rod butt reaches 12 o'clock, level with your ear, it is stopped. This stopping of the rod's backward-drive is caused by squeezing the butt with the thumb as if it were a tennis ball in the palm of the hand.

It follows that this stopping of the rod has anchored the spring, but, being a spring, the rest of the rod from the butt up to the tip flexes backwards, firstly driven by your muscular power, and secondly pulled back at the tip by the heavy line unfurling behind you. This stores up the spring's energy.

There's a critical pause to allow the line to extend to the rear and to pull against the rod tip. Then the rod is driven forwards again to the place from which it started its power arc, which is 10.30. But this time the spring's energy is released, pushing the line out in front of you, and as it shoots out so it turns over until you have a perfectly straight line over the water. It then begins to fall as its energy is spent, followed down by the rod tip to a normal fishing height of about 9 o'clock.

Thus we have two simple movements with a pause between. Before the back cast really starts, the line has to be slid gently from the water, gradually speeding up, but, consulting out time-piece, you will see that the power arc is actually quite short. These two parts of the power arc, plus the pause between, must be practised until a reasonably straight line can be laid out without effort.

Use of the Wrist

When the first stages of casting have been mastered the wrist does come into play, but this is essentially different, because it now controls the rod, giving it extra snap to speed the line on its way. This involves the wrist being cocked forwards on the back-cast, so that it actually travels behind the forearm. Then, at the end of the back-cast, it uncocks, only to snap forward again as the rod starts its forward drive. This usually develops naturally with casting ability, so the learner needn't worry about it. The position is shown in the diagram.

Use of the Left Hand

Until now, you have been casting with a fixed length of line. As soon as you can control this and lay it out in a straight line, you will wish to extend your distance. This is normally done by false casting, which means that instead of allowing the line to fall in front we move it backward again, keeping it always in the air.

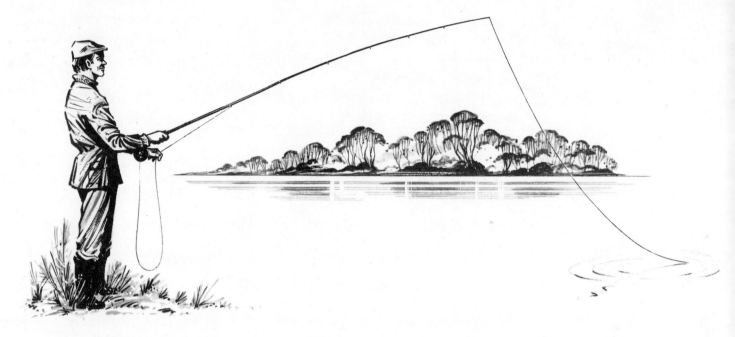

Overhead cast 1: rod slightly
raised, left hand gently pulls
line to free it from water
adhesion

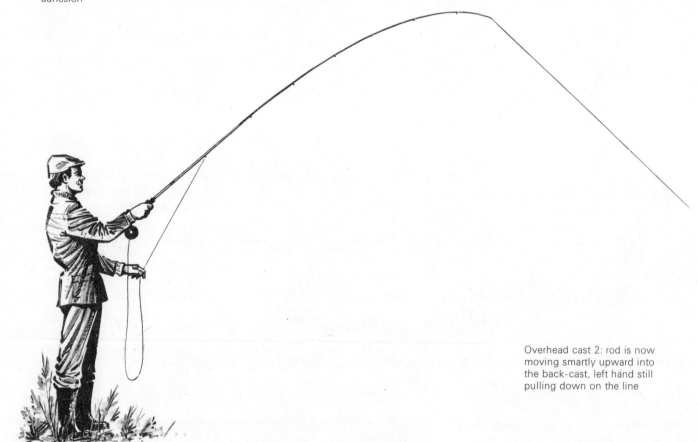

Overhead cast 2: rod is now
moving smartly upward into
the back-cast, left hand still
pulling down on the line

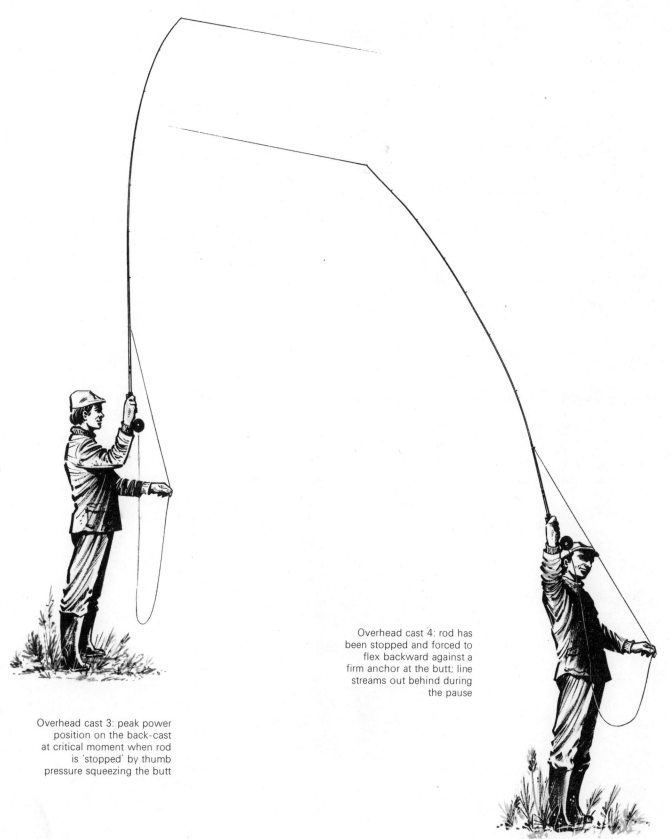

Overhead cast 4: rod has
been stopped and forced to
flex backward against a
firm anchor at the butt; line
streams out behind during
the pause

Overhead cast 3: peak power
position on the back-cast
at critical moment when rod
is 'stopped' by thumb
pressure squeezing the butt

Overhead cast 5: the line having straightened behind, the rod now drives forward again; left hand still keeps line taut

Overhead cast 6: Termination of the forward cast: line unfurls over the water, left hand releases line into the shoot

Final position for fishing out
the cast, with rod at a
comfortable angle for striking
and starting the next
back-cast

At two points in the false cast, the moving line pulls hard against the rod tip. This is at the final extensions of the backward and forward cast. At these climaxes, a further yard or two of line can be fed into the air from the reel, and distance gradually extended. This is known as shooting line, but the line has to be pulled from the reel by the left hand. Now, instead of pinching the line against the rod butt, take it between the forefinger and thumb of the left hand. During the back-cast, pull down the line towards your left hip, taking some line from the reel and some through the rings from the airborne line. On the extension of the line behind you, allow the extra reel-line to slip through your fingers. The same action can also be performed on the forward-cast.

At the same time, two further qualities will have been introduced into your casting. Firstly, you will be able to increase the distance of your cast, and secondly, you are able to increase the speed of the line in the air. False casting also helps you to measure off a cast to a given point or fish by watching how far it goes over the target, and it's also used for drying a floating fly that has become waterlogged.

Stance

In fishing, how you stand is often dictated by physical conditions. Normally, a fairly open, relaxed position is the best. The snag of advancing one foot and shoulder in front of the other is that it can throw the line off course, even causing the hook to foul the cast in the air. When timing goes astray, it's useful to be able to turn the head to follow the line to the rear, which means left-foot forward, but the habit should be abandoned when timing settles down again.

Rod Plane

This, too, is dictated by fishing conditions. The ideal should be the upright rod, but many of us, used to casting on windswept banks, tend to lay the rod away from the body. The reason is that a long line may be carried by a wayward breeze behind the caster's head with the hook coming into the neck or ear.

Errors

Bearing in mind the positive approach, there are one or two essential points to guard against. The commonest mistake is known as the 'wrist break'. The novice has no casting muscles and so the rod takes control of his weaker wrist. Instead of being able to stop the rod at the vertical position, as described,

Wrist hinging backward under rod pressure, allowing energy to be dissipated from the 'rod-spring'. The illustration shows a common error in that the butt has moved too far away from the forearm

the flexing action forces the wrist to break backward. As the spring's energy leaks away, the caster compensates by applying physical effort. The trouble is that such a caster never learns what a fly rod feels like when it's doing its job.

The remedy sounds easy enough. Don't let the rod compel the wrist to hinge backwards. Alas, until a deal of casting has been done, the wrist may be too weak to resist the power of the rod, the more reason not to have too big a rod to learn with. The easiest way to overcome this, while learning, and thus to get the feel of a working rod, is to push the rod butt up the sleeve, or even to use straps or wide rubber bands around rod-butt and wrist.

The check-point is to see if the end of the rod butt moves away from the wrist during the back cast. This throws the strain onto the forearm and shoulder which are strong enough to resist the wish of the rod to stray back beyond the vertical. The encouraging thing is that this fault is the cause of at least 80% of casting error, and once it has been overcome the overhead cast has been virtually mastered.

Timing

Timing is one of those mysteries, like balance, which can hardly be taught by an outsider. In casting, the pause which allows the line to extend behind is the bugbear. Too short a pause, the fly cracks off, too long and the line hits the ground behind or loses all of its momentum. Fortunately this one is easily cured. You advance the left foot slightly so that you can turn your head to watch the line extend behind. As it does so, you start the forward drive of the rod butt. The only snag is that as you turn there's a tendency to throw the line across its true path, but this is of no great matter in short-line practice. Later, you will detect the subtle pull of the extended line against the rod tip.

Conclusions

Instruction is difficult for the beginner, for unlike most sports we lack recognised, competent teachers. The day may come when we emulate other sports and appoint instructors to our fisheries, as has been done at Sundridge Lake, in Kent. At present this is a rare event, and it's difficult to answer why we lack this facility in fly fishing. It is to do with the individuality of anglers, the history of the way our sport has developed. We shall have the casting clinic and the 'pro shop service', as they do in the U.S.A. because fly-fishing interest is literally exploding in Britain as vast, new reservoirs are stocked with trout. It may be hard to learn casting from this book, or any other, but it can be done.

Above all, regard the rod as a spring and compel it to work, to wind up on the back-cast, release its pent-up power on the forward-cast. Don't let it call the tune to your wrist. Stiff-wristed casting feels clumsy, but it does bring out the fly rod's action.

Distance Casting

Distance casting is the aim of the bank fisherman on trout reservoirs, especially when he has to contend with extensive shallows, crowded areas or lakes where fish have been driven from the margins by careless wading. It is also useful for the man who fishes on broad rivers.

Two Options

For extra yards, we are faced with two choices: to achieve the maximum with normal fly-fishing gear, or to use the shooting head. Whatever system we plump for, the vital thing is to avoid the tempting error that you have to beef up the tackle and use more power. The result is that you will quickly wear yourself out, reaching less distance than you did with your lighter, normal outfit. So make up your mind to gain extra distance within a tackle system suited to your physique.

Let's examine the secret of distance casting. Given that an average angler can keep in the air only a comfortable length of line, say 15 yards, it follows that the remainder has to be 'shot', or pulled out by the speed of the line in the air at the extension of the forward-cast. In other words, the secret of distance casting is line speed.

Distance with Normal Gear

It's a fallacy to suppose that you necessarily need more powerful tackle to increase line speed. You may be able to achieve better results within your existing outfit. The factors that speed line are obvious – rod action, line weight, reduced line drag through the rings and casting technique. Obviously, if you already have a slow-tipped rod, one with a soggy butt-action, then you do need one with a crisper tip movement. A longer rod, by itself, may often have a slower tip speed.

The trouble with line weight is that as you increase it, so do you bring in various nasty side effects. If you overload your existing rod, the action will become floppy. If you harness a heavy line to a fast-tipped rod you may have much trouble in controlling its fierce turnover.

You may well reduce drag through the rod rings in two ways, firstly by fitting new rings, unflawed, which you may gently polish, and secondly by raising the rod butt as you shoot the final line, so that it doesn't have to climb up a steep hill to reach the tip-ring. Bear in mind, too, that line drag can come from the ground or water on which the shooting line is lying.

Double-haul

Now we come to casting technique, which, for distance work, means the 'double haul'. Basically, this is two left-hand hauls of line with a feed-back between them, the first haul coinciding with the back-cast, the second haul with the forward cast, and the feed-back happens as the line extends behind

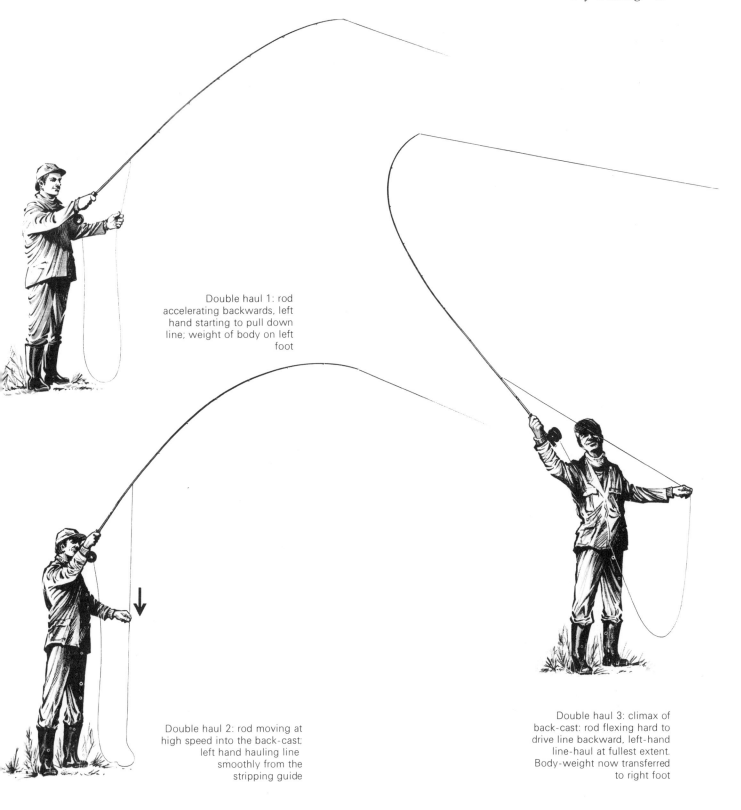

Double haul 1: rod accelerating backwards, left hand starting to pull down line; weight of body on left foot

Double haul 2: rod moving at high speed into the back-cast; left hand hauling line smoothly from the stripping guide

Double haul 3: climax of back-cast: rod flexing hard to drive line backward, left-hand line-haul at fullest extent. Body-weight now transferred to right foot

Double haul 4: line is fully
extended behind, with rod
drifting back behind caster's
shoulder. Left hand feeds line
back through the rod rings
without letting go

Double haul 5:
commencement of the
forward power drive: caster
begins to sweep the rod
forward as left hand starts to
pull line through the guides

Double haul 6: maximum
effort on the forward cast:
rod flexing hard to drive line
out, left hand still hauling
line downward, body weight
now swinging back on to
left foot

Double haul 7: the climax of the cast, with rod checked, line streaming out and unrolling over the water in the 'shoot' released by left hand

on the culmination of the back cast. I deliberately said 'basically' as there are some subtleties of timing, yet to be explained.

Let's look at the rod movement first. We've noted already that while it's sensible to think of the fly rod as a simple spring, we do add leverage, particularly in distance casting. To allow room for leverage and time for these two hauls and feed-back, the rod drifts back beyond the classical, vertical right-ear position at the climax of the back-cast. The trouble is that it must be still wound up, and if it were allowed to drift back weakly there would be no pent-up energy in the rod to help drive the line forwards again.

The controlled drift back of the rod behind the shoulder is hard to describe, though it's quite easy to 'feel'. When the rod is thrown backwards smartly, reaching the vertical position, the butt is 'squeezed' rather than stopped. The rod flexes backward against the resistance of the wrist and forearm, while the elbow and shoulder joints hinge to allow the rod to drift backwards.

In other words, we still keep a short, fierce power-arc, rod-spring winding up against the wrist, but the rod is, at the same time, flowing sweetly backwards over a longer arc. The wrist's stopping power is applied through a strong squeezing action of the hand on the butt, especially in pushing the thumb into the cork butt.

Wrist Action

To complicate the written word, at least, the wrist is not entirely rigid. It is cocked forward at the start of the back-cast, gives a controlled backward flip after the rod has flexed on the cast and then snaps forward during the forward-cast to add considerable tip-speed to the rod. These factors, taken individually in print, sound complicated, but the illustrations will help to give a basic correct technique and the actions should develop themselves. They are far easier to apply physically than to describe in words.

Body Position

Body action is necessary in distance casting and some of the larger back muscles are brought into play. I cast with my left-foot advanced so that my head turns to follow the path of the line on the back cast, at least until I have the timing right. It also allows the rod to clear the body with ease, giving free movement of the rod. The arm is also free to lift, hinge and move freely, and the right shoulder can swing into the forward cast, punching the rod through. This is for that extra leverage that's so essential. Perhaps the most important reason for this stance is to permit the transferrance of weight on to the rear foot during the back-cast, then on to the front-foot on the forward-cast. These should be gentle shifts of weight, not violent rockings backward and forward, which would set up commotion in the water.

The Casting Action

The purpose of describing these body movements and rod arcs before the actual casting action is to avoid confusion in the sequence. Get this sequence right, the rest will slot into place.

With either line or shooting head before you, a small left-hand pull clears surface adhesion, the rod accelerates backwards as the left hand pulls line down from the butt rod-ring.

The rod reaches the vertical, the butt is given a 'squeeze' against which the rod flexes while it drifts less strongly backwards. The line streams out behind, encouraging the left hand to feed back line through the rings, and in so doing the left hand will come up near to the rod ring.

The rod drives forwards again after this pause, feed-back and line extension, while the left hand again pulls down line. The line drives forward over the water, when the left hand releases its own line for the final shoot. Two or three such sequences can be built before the final shoot is made, as it were, a sort of 'double haul false casting' in which the left hand never releases line until the climax.

Timing

The thing we all notice in double-hauling, as in the golf swing, is that once in a while we hit the perfect timing and the line just zooms out like a rocket. Evidently, timing has to be felt rather than described.

The left-hand hauls should never be fierce or jerky, but gentle and sweetly-flowing into each other. Vigorous, jerky hauls dissipate line-speed. The two timing problems are exactly when to start the hauls and when to release the line for the shoot. The beginner will find it helps to start the hauls exactly when the rod starts to move into the power arc. Later, he will find it may vary from rod to rod. My 'Two Lakes' prefers the second to start fractionally before the rod begins to move, but slow-actioned rods required a slightly delayed haul.

You should experiment, varying this timing slightly until you are able to 'groove' your timing into muscle-memory. And remember, as with the normal, overhead cast, wind direction and strength affects hauls in exactly the same way.

Now for the timing of the shoot. 'Feel' is again the key. There will be a moment when your casting projectile takes off from the rod tip and just begs for a free reign – let it go! It usually happens as it turns over fairly close to the water, in ideal conditions, but a wind in your face spells out a later line release and a wind in your neck requires it earlier. Rehearse in various directions and speeds of wind.

Faults and Checks

The great danger from describing stages of a cast in word and picture is that it tends to freeze the images in the mind into static positions, whereas a cast is a mobile, living thing. Try to apply the general concept without thinking of a particular position or body part at any given time, for you will emphasise this to the ruin of the whole. This is also the trouble with faults. Build up a positive concept of the whole cast, and do not visualise a series of unconnected responses to faults.

This is the massive error in all physical routines for all sports. We teach negatively. A positive concept of the cast in its entirety will wipe out faults as you build it up, but if you concentrate on correcting one fault in the routine, the rest of it will fall to pieces. In short, think positively!

Specialised Fly Casts

Although the idea of developing specialised casts is at first daunting, they are mostly constructed on the normal fly-cast to deal with special circumstances, such as wind, or high obstacles behind.

The most dangerous winds for the reservoir bank fisherman is the one which carries the fly behind his head on the back cast, which, for the right-hander is the breeze blowing into his right ear. If the rod follows its usual upright path the line may be swept leftwards as it goes behind the angler and the hook is nicely lined-up for the back of the neck! The remedy is to lay the rod over the the right, slantwise, allowing plenty of room for the line to come through between the rod's path and the right shoulder.

The wind blowing in the opposite direction, that is into the left ear, carries no such danger, but it has the effect of making the cast fizzle out. Again, this is simply because the line is swept off course and cannot drive straight forward and turn over. My remedy here is not to throw the line behind the head on the back-cast, for winds are famous for their waywardness. I change the whole direction of the cast, diagonally across the wind, turning both shoulders and body half-right. In this way, the line picks up some of the wind like a sail, and goes with it. The most bothersome winds of all are the squally airs from straight in front of you. When you come to think of it, though, there's not so much trouble with the back-cast, but because this wind takes the line behind you with ease you fail to apply enough power.

This is when you need power most, to wind up the rod for a good forward punch. The trick of casting into the wind is quite simple: the idea is to imagine you are trying to throw the line under the wind. In other words, you delay the forward shoot of line, then push it through low and hard, close to the surface of the water.

Of course, you usually get a slap-down of line if the wind is strong, but at least you reach a fair distance. If you are double-hauling, then delay the second-line haul until half-way through the rod's forward movement. The line bowls out in a vicious, narrow loop. You will need to check constantly for wind-knots in the leader, but you'll be astonished at how successfully the line goes out. Two other points are essential: keep the elbow low, near to your side; a long, straight arm is hopeless when casting into the wind. And uncock the wrist a little on the back-cast, then snap it forward fractionally before you shoot line through the rings.

Few people realise that a wind from behind is quite tricky because it stops the line pulling the rod-tip backward, and thus the spring is wound up poorly. When the wind is in the back of your neck, really punch that rod on the back-cast. Now for obstacles. On reservoirs these may be high walls of the dam, or even a barbed-wire fence. Trees are rare, but sloping banks with long grass or bushes are the devil for the long line merchant. It is our English tradition to throw the line back, straight and hard, whereas Americans adopt a much higher back-cast than us as a result of their preference for light, short rods.

An American angler I know throws his rod up from the shoulder on the back-cast, so that the arm is still, straight up in one line to the rod-tip. At the same time he pulls down hard with the left hand. The line goes in a high angle above his right shoulder (the so-called 'steeple cast'). He then has to change the direction of the forward-cast, driving the line out over the water in the usual way. It's this change of line direction which gave the steeple cast the bad reputation of being splashy. This is unfair. It's only lack of practice that causes the bad delivery. Work at the 'steeple' and you will find you can drop the fly like thistledown, the trick being to aim at an imaginary point above the surface. You can also get a reasonable distance. This is the cast for those concrete walls and wire fences.

Once I'd mastered steeple casting the roll cast became almost obsolete for me, necessitating as it must a change of direction with each cast – roll out a few, you'll see what I mean. Roll casting is very easy, as it only involves building up a line belly behind the shoulder by sweetly raising the rod tip. The rod is then cut down smartly, bowling the line out like a hoop. This hoop snakes along the line, turns the leader over, jerks the fly into the air and dumps it out in front of you. The spring of the rod is wound up by the weight of the belly of the line, flexing the rod against the stickiness of the fly line on or in the water. It's great with a double-handed salmon rod, but I don't care for it with a trout rod.

A word about gear – the casting of a line into the wind is difficult unless the leader is balanced to the line. I make up a storm-leader, short and steeply tapered. It is necessary to avoid too big a step-down in thickness between fly line point and leader-butt. It goes without saying that this wind coming into the bank of a big reservoir will raise quite a lop, even eroding the bank and turning the near water quite cloudy. In such conditions I use a large, gay fly. Three sections of nylon to a total length of 7 ft. is quite adequate, from a butt of 18. b.s. to a point of 12. b.s. as line visibility is no problem to the fish swimming in coffee.

We complain about wind and obstacles until we meet the most irritating combination of all – the complete absence of both. Imagine yourself on an open bank, silhouetted against the sky with the water brilliant and calm before you. Here we need the lightest fall of fly possible. The line is kept high on the forward-cast, the power is also turned off early with rod tip holding the line back in its fall to the surface so that fly and leader aren't brought down with a wallop. The flies settle gently, pierce the surface film if lightly dressed, and the retrieve should aim at making no visible wake from the knots.

We cannot avoid all line flash and shadow, but we can certainly eliminate rod flash. The high gloss finish on modern reservoir fly rods is quite silly and is there only for display. Such rods can emit sunbeams across the whole width of Chew lake. It's a poor tribute to our intelligence that rod makers feel they have to satisfy our aesthetic taste at the expense of good fishing, but fly lines also suffer from the same fault. I leave the rubbing down to you, but you can buy glitter-free leaders and nylon. Strange that the quality needed to sell a leader is exactly the opposite of that needed, or rather what some anglers think is needed, for a line or rod. In 1914 the French army had much élan, attacking in bright blue coats and red pantaloons, but camouflage later saved overwork by German machine-gunners. The trout will not see us if we bear that in mind.

The Steeple Cast

The aim of the 'steeple cast' is a high line on the back-cast to avoid obstacles behind. The angle of the line is changed on the forward-cast so that it is driven out above the water.

The back-cast begins with the right arm extended straight in front of the caster. The left hand holds line near to the bottom rod ring, called the 'stripping guide', and just before the rod is pushed upwards into the back-cast, the line is pulled down from the ring to unstick it from the water's adhesion.

The rod and the entire casting arm are lifted smartly together as one piece and stopped strongly at the vertical while, simultaneously the left hand is hauling the line downwards from the stripping guide. The line flies upwards from the rod tip, streaming high on the back cast. The extension pause is shorter than in the overhead cast.

At the start of the back cast, the wrist is cocked forwards. At the moment the forward drive begins, the wrist snaps backwards to allow for a change of angle in the line's direction. Then the rod is pushed forwards with a pronounced snap of the wrist. Although this sounds complex, when attempting the 'steeple cast', the changed direction of the line on the forward-cast will actually compel the caster to make the necessary changes in wrist and arm movements, otherwise the line will simply thrash down on to the water, in a heap. The whole secret of steeple casting is the concept of the arm as a straight extension of the rod.

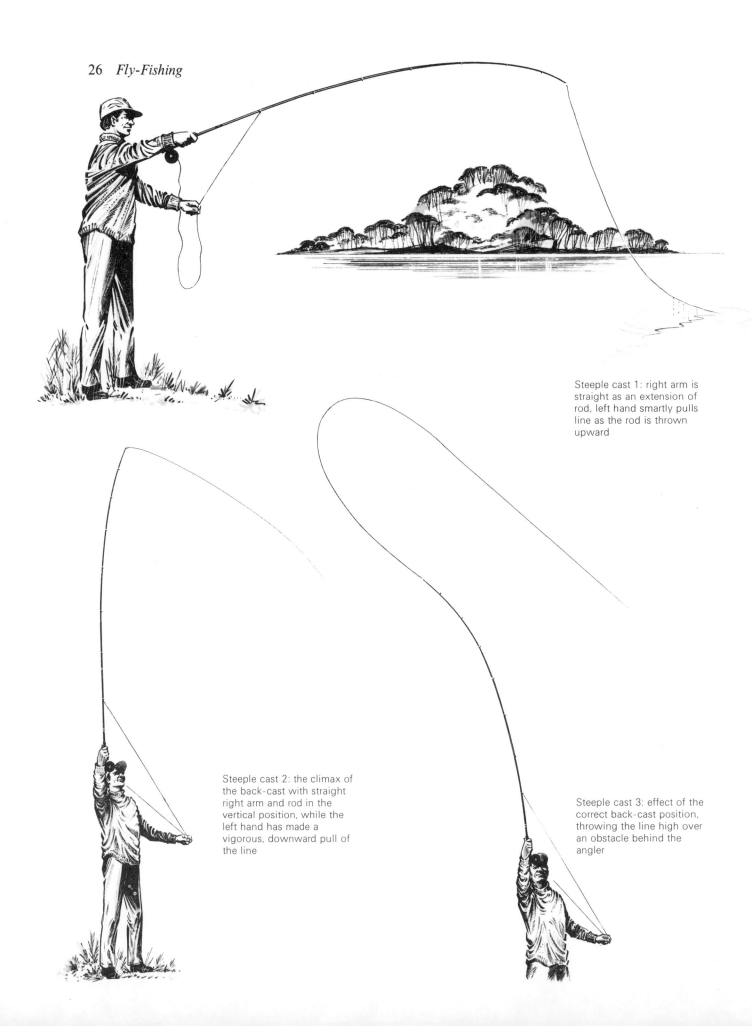

Steeple cast 1: right arm is straight as an extension of rod, left hand smartly pulls line as the rod is thrown upward

Steeple cast 2: the climax of the back-cast with straight right arm and rod in the vertical position, while the left hand has made a vigorous, downward pull of the line

Steeple cast 3: effect of the correct back-cast position, throwing the line high over an obstacle behind the angler

Steeple cast 4: final movement and shoot of the
steeple cast. As the line is
driven out, the rod is also
pushed forward to change
the angle of the line and
unroll it over the water

The Roll Cast

The roll cast is the easiest one of all! Its purpose is to deal with really high obstacles immediately behind – fences, walls and the like, where even the steeple cast wouldn't work.

With the line extended in front of the caster, the rod is raised gently while the left hand pulls line down wards from the stripping guide at matching speed. The rod-arm can be raised fairly high as the rod comes toward the vertical. The rod is taken sweetly backwards, without check until a belly of line falls in a curve from the rod tip behind the shoulder. This is the essential position for starting the forward-cast, which is a sudden snap down of the rod, bowling the line over the water, so that the leader turns over to drop the fly in a straight line.

The line on the back-cast is on the outside of both the rod and the shoulder. Because of this we encounter the main problem of a succession of roll casts, which is that they enforce a change of direction to the right with each line extension. In river fishing, this means the line is moving downstream further with each cast, which is usually overcome by moving down the pool a yard or so between each cast or two, regathering line to start the next series of roll casts.

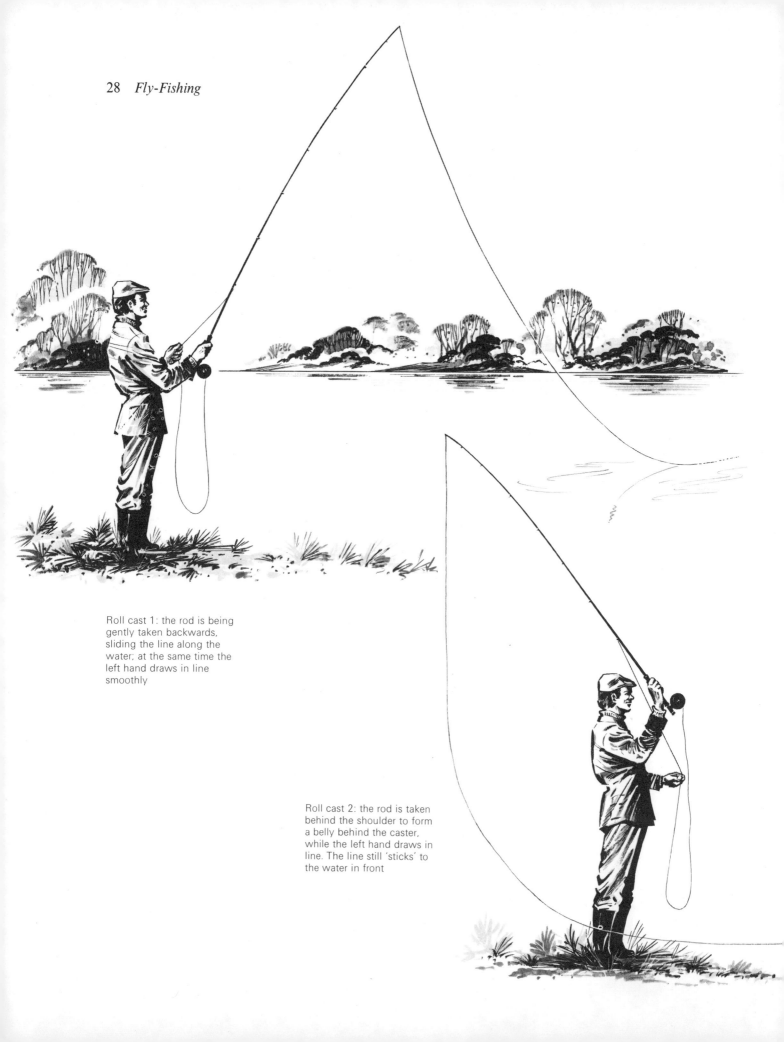

Roll cast 1: the rod is being gently taken backwards, sliding the line along the water; at the same time the left hand draws in line smoothly

Roll cast 2: the rod is taken behind the shoulder to form a belly behind the caster, while the left hand draws in line. The line still 'sticks' to the water in front

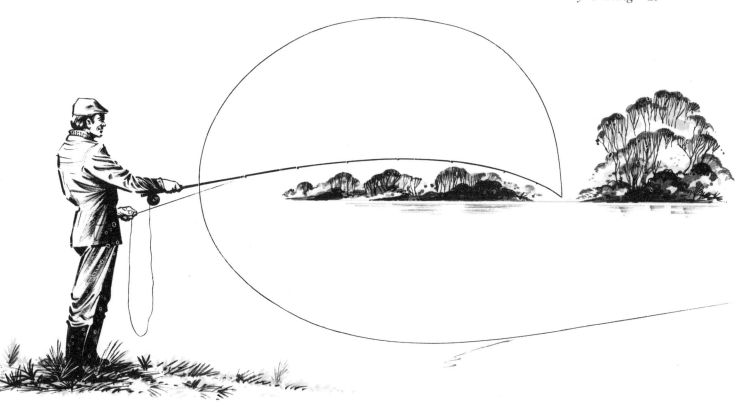

Roll cast 3: the rod now snaps downwards, driving the line forward and over the water in a hoop

The Side Cast

This cast is simply an overhead cast laid on its side. It has two purposes, firstly to push a line under a tunnel of trees, and secondly to drop a dry fly leader in a Shepherd's Crook shape so that the nylon cannot come down over the trout's head before the fly. This latter point is an essential refinement on heavily fished dry-fly waters, and to it we can add a further argument – that a moving line, close to the water, alarms fish far less than one flashing high in the air. The cast is far more useful than might seem apparent at first, for it's especially accurate in putting a fly to a fish close to an irregular bank, as when a tussock or bush intervenes between you and the fish.

Obviously the rod is laid over, parallel to the water, and the back-cast can be followed visually. The wrist is used more in side casting, and the temptation to make too large a power-arc must be resisted. These casts are usually short, from below a fish, so the cast must be crisp and restrained. Fine judgement is needed to stop the rod on the forward-cast to prevent the line overshooting and to bring the fly into the right drift-path of the fish.

It's a valuable cast to use across a fast current to counteract drag, since the line falls unevenly and the current takes time to form a belly, which causes the fly to skate.

Side cast 1: the rod is kept
low and parallel to the
water. Left hand draws in
line and the rod and reel are
tilted inward before cast is
made

Side cast 2: the rod is thrown
sideways, line streams
backwards over the water
and straightens when rod is
'stopped'. Head turns to
follow path of line

Side cast 3: rod drives
forwards, still parallel to the
water, and when the energy
of the line is spent it's
allowed to fall by its own
weight

Geoffrey Bucknall
demonstrates the second
position of the side-cast

Ambidextrous Casting

It's been assumed that the caster is right-handed, and all instructions may simply be reversed for left-handed anglers. Left-handed casting used to cause wonder at exhibitions, yet it's fairly easy to master and is of great value to the river angler.

An obvious advantage is that it opens up more vantage points from which to attack a trout. When trout have been in a river for quite some time the 'easy' ones have all been killed long since, while those protected by obstacles or drag remain secure. Worn patches of bank testify where the habitual right-hander has cast to each wary old-timer. By changing bank and making left-handed casts such fish will see the fly in an entirely different way – free. The trick is to use the right hand to teach the left, using two identical fly outfits, one in each hand, with a reasonable length of line. Raise both rods together, establishing a rhythm between them, until the left-side muscles develop and the arm takes up the correct routine from the right. Now discard the 'master' and continue with the left hand alone, while the right takes the line from reel to stripping guide, which may, by the way, prove to be the hardest part to learn.

Two-handed Casting

This is the cast with the long salmon rods. When the length of the fly rod exceeds ten feet, for most casters it becomes increasingly difficult to manage. Some rods between ten and eleven feet have a screw-in butt attachment to increase their length and to convert them for two-handed use. Beyond eleven feet, their design is invariably with the long butt, reel position at the bottom, for two-handed casting.

It's possible that the long, two-handed rods will decline in popularity with the modern improvements in performance of single-handed rods. British casters are stubborn traditionalists, and on our torrential Highland rivers in particular, nothing else can 'hang' a fly in the current so effectively as the long rod, held fairly high. For this reason, plus a personal love for the brutes, I include this short section on two-handed casting.

Probably the man who first takes up a long salmon rod will already have experienced the single-handed trout rod and is seeking to extend his range. The long rod should have no terror for him; the casting mechanics are the same, that of driving the rod back against an anchor to 'wind it up'. This time, though, the anchor is the two hands of the caster, not the single wrist.

The casting grip is with the right hand holding the butt firmly above the reel, comfortably near to the top of the cork handle. The left hand loosely cups the end of the handle, and this is quite a light hold. I must say that my own preference is for a left-hand hold below the reel, but round the cork handle, not cupping the end of the rod. The reason is that I can squeeze the reel-line against the handle, shooting extra line when I need more distance.

When a trout man first casts with the long salmon rod he finds to his dismay that the line falls very low on the back-cast. He is constantly flicking off points of expensive salmon flies on the rocks behind. This is the two-handed equivalent of the weak wrist-hinge in trout casting, but with the salmon-casting error we say that the two hands are working against each other. The fault has the same basic cause of the rod compelling the untutored muscles to release tension under pressure. The right hand is pulled backwards and the left-hand pushes forwards in a see-saw action which feels quite sensible . . . until you feel your fly tug on the ground behind you.

The old-time preventive was to hook the forefinger of the left-hand into the top button-hole of the coat while casting. It had the dual virtue of preventing the sea-saw energy leak, while ensuring that the rod-butt was nice and high throughout the cast. I prefer to put across the mental image of the rod acting as a spring so that we can grasp the need for a firm anchor-plate of the back-cast. Also, I prefer to keep both my hands further in front of my body, say about a foot from my chest, so that I can lift the whole rod as one piece, without rocking the two hands against each other.

Two-handed casting is much easier than the single-handed trout cast. It would probably be more sensible to teach novices with the salmon rod because the essential flexing action of the fly rod is more easily felt, and the rod flexing backwards is more readily stopped with two hands than with one wrist. Once the trout caster has overcome the low line on the back-cast he has very little trouble with salmon-fly casting. The trout roll cast is easily translated to a salmon rod, with its copious line belly behind the shoulder, and its longer driving arc. I have to think that two-handed casting is much the easiest technique of the two, and once the rôle of the two hands is understood and mastered the salmon rod can really be enjoyed.

True, there's a different feel, the sheer slow ease with which the spring unwinds on the forward-cast in comparison with trout rods, the action of which is snappier now than in the past. There are adjustments to be made, such as resisting the temptation to thrash the line down because it seems so slow in coming through. Work down a wide river, and if the basic technique is right, the adjustments come along on their own and you will feel that pleasure of leisurely unfurling the line over the water, without the tension and pace that many casters write into their trout fishing under the mistaken impression that this is the key to the distance race.

There are, then, two factors to guard against when converting to the long salmon rod: firstly the rod's compulsion to pull forward your left-hand and push back your right. And secondly the great time lag in all of the line's responses to the rod's movements.

Still Life

2 Tackle

Casting is described first, before the actual tackle, because we need to know what we must do before considering the implements.

In casting, we visualise the rod as a simple spring. The spring has certain lengths according to its purpose, very short, say seven feet for fishing narrow streams which wrinkle the moors, and quite long, up to fourteen feet, for salmon fishing on the great flows rushing to pour into the oceans. Between these limits are the work-horses, the rods for all-round use on normal streams and lakes.

The spring has certain actions, which is a choice of speeds at which it unwinds, such as the fast whiplash of the dry-fly fisherman, swiftly intercepting a trout cruising on the surface, or the gentle arc of the boat-angler's rod, absorbing the sudden lunge of a hefty rainbow at close range on a tight line and fine nylon leader.

The everyday work-horse of fly fishing is the nine-foot rod of medium action. It doubles up for occasional interludes of specialised casting, such as bank-fishing on a vast reservoir. The man who lives close to a certain type of fishery will obviously own a specialised fly rod to suit his commonest method. Leaving that aside for the moment, what will an average nine-footer cope with?

It will fish the wet and dry fly on medium-sized rivers. It is suited to boat fishing on lakes and reservoirs. It stands up to distance casting from the banks of reservoirs, though a specialised rod may be preferred. It is used on the smaller, often private trout lakes in Britain. It can be applied to the odd trip to a sea-trout river, and even handle salmon on smaller streams. Therefore it has a wide range of capability.

The specialised rods I use are a short seven-footer for fishing on small brooks, a limber ten-footer for boat fishing, a more powerful nine-footer for distance casting on reservoirs, and a double-handed salmon fly rod of twelve feet. We will have another look at these rods after a short discussion on the materials from which they are made.

Today, most fly rods are made from hollow fibre-glass. A few years ago built-cane was the most popular material, and perhaps the minority who still prefer it do so because we have a tendency in fly-fishing to rush new developments on to the market before they are perfected. The early glass rods were poor in comparison to cane, and some of that mud still sticks. Modern glass rods may outclass cane models, though I can understand the love for the traditional, craftsman-built tool. A cane fly rod does have a certain sweetness that no synthetic material captures, but from a practical viewpoint, glass, because of its strength and lightness, is the obvious choice.

Nowadays we make fly rods with glass-to-glass ferrules, eliminating the dead-spots in rod-action caused by the old-fashioned brass ferrules. The usual spigot is a section of tapered glass cemented into the lower joint and on to which the higher section fits. Being tapered, a correctly fitted spigot allows for a gap of $\frac{1}{4}$ in. or so between the two rod sections, and it is quite wrong to force the top joint down hard in an attempt to mate-up the two. The spigot should hold its higher section quite firmly; extra pressure will split the glass.

The rod fittings are personal preferences, albeit based on practical reasons. I have discarded the rubber button on the butt which added weight and prefer a screw winch fitting to hold the reel, one which screws the reel seats toward the end of the rod rather than towards the cork-handle; this is for balance and comfort. I like my cork-handle to flair outwards at the top end as this assists my 'thumb-squeeze' method of 'stopping' the rod on the back-cast. My lowest rod ring is made of tungsten-carbide steel which never grooves, while the intermediate rings are stainless steel snakes, hugging the line against the rod. The tip-ring is a wide-diameter hard-chromed steel ring.

Design Factors

In 1966 I was experimenting with the light shooting head for distance fly-casting as opposed to the then prevailing 'longbow' type of rod with its long line in the air. As it was a challenge to established tackle and methods there was considerable opposition, but, worse, since there was no basis for new casting methods in Britain at that time, there was equally no specialised tackle for the new experimentation. Everything had to be improvised. Since then I've been fortunate enough to produce and market a fly rod for the new light-shooting head casting system, a rod which took its name from the famous fishery, 'Two Lakes', where it had been put through its paces against giant rainbow and brown trout. Literally thousands of this rod-design have since passed into the hands of anglers. What was the secret?

By coincidence, the fastish dry-fly action is also the best for building up speed quickly to cast a light shooting head. So by constructing a rod with this action in just under 9 ft. of hollow glass to cast a normal size 6 double-taper line, we had the ideal medium for throwing shorter shooting heads cut from size 7 and 8 lines. Exactly what shooting heads are will be explained later, but basically, we are dealing with a projectile hurled out by a fast rod action.

We added next an orthodox 9 ft. 6 in. reservoir fly rod for the traditional caster with his long line in the air. It was a commercial exercise, and while it performed its task admirably I was slightly unhappy a concession had been made to the past. We had fallen into the old error of equating rod power with rod length. We should have learned from the Americans, and later I did.

We do not need to increase the length of the rod to handle a heavier line for casting further. By varying the taper we can make any action and line-loading within, say, 9 ft. of glass. And by tightening up the taper at this rod length I realised I could give to a size 8 line the same tip speed that the Two Lakes rod gave to the shooting head. The resulting rod was the 'Powercast', and even I found it difficult to believe reports of average casters putting out an entire 30 yard line, until I saw it for myself. It must be admitted, though, that this rod was coupled to a specially designed fly line with reduced friction area behind its belly. I used to believe that almost any fly rod would be suitable for boat fishing. Dreaming on a calm drift in a sultry afternoon at Chew, this huge rainbow snatched the Peter Ross close to the boat. Immediately he hurled himself into the sky, hanging for a fraction of time, motionless at the summit of his leap, every scarlet spot glaring at me, like open wounds . . . then the hook came away, because the rod was too stiff to absorb the sudden shock on a tight line. This unhappy moment conceived my 'Bobfly' rod, 10 ft. of supple glass contented with only a size 6 line. The top dropper-fly can be dibbled capriciously in the surface film. The rod even doubles up for dapping, and that limber action will absorb the impact of a charging fish at close range.

A longer rod is also useful for sea-trout fishing, the gentle action being kind to the hook-hold in the soft mouth of this migrant from the ocean. The extra inches keep the line high about bankside vegetation, for there's no surer way to ruin a pool at night than by clambering in and out of the water to free snagged line.

Many fishing conditions offer choices of rod. Take the meandering brook: you can either wade right down in it with a wand-like brook rod, uncurling the line under overhanging tree branches, or you can keep your distance from the bank, using a long rod to throw a high line over the tops of the undergrowth.

Finally, we come to the heavy guns, the salmon rods. In Britain and Scandinavia the two-handers are still popular, though in America there seems to be a preference for using single-handed rods of greater power for the same conditions. Certainly you can scale down a salmon rod, settling for a length of $11\frac{1}{2}$ ft. with a sliding winch fitting, which allows you to position the reel exactly where you wish on the butt. I've made my own taper slightly tougher, to throw a longer line, and the rod is ideal for the smaller and medium salmon rivers, like the lower Towey, Teifi, Taw, Torridge and those on the Scottish border, where you feel comfortable with the extra power yet don't require the all-out resources of the traditional salmon rod.

To recapitulate, most beginners should start with a rod within their physical resources, bearing in mind their untried muscles. The actual weight of the rod is no guide to its fatigue-factor. The thing that makes you tired is the effort required to flex the rod, to drive it back against the anchor of the wrist. The so-called 'reservoir' rods would probably give less distance to a tired novice after an hour's casting than, say, a light nine-footer of my own 'Two Lakes' type. Specialised rods can be added to the armoury later.

As we have seen, the colour and finish of the rod are important. I was convinced by the argument of G. E. M. Skues, one of the early masters of dry-fly technique and originator of the upstream nymph method of trout fishing, that a light grey is the least visible colour against the sky. He would have painted all his rods that colour had it not been for the tremendous weight of those old-fashioned enamels in his time. You can have your glass rods impregnated without extra weight. Regarding finish, so many times have I seen fish bolting from the flash of a highly varnished rod in sunlight that I insist on a dull finish for my own rods. I achieve this by putting on one layer of normal gloss varnish to seal the glass, followed by two coats of matt-varnish to remove any trace of flash. Glossy rods are beautiful in cabinets.

Fly Lines

We know that the artificial fly is virtually weightless, which is why we have our combination of rod-spring and line weight to put the fly where we want it. We have seen that part of the rod's flexing action is caused by the caster's actions. Another cause is the weight of the line pulling the rod tip backwards, against the anchoring wrist, on the back-cast, and forward again. This weight has to suit the power of the rod. If it is too little, then the line cannot pull the rod tip back far enough on the back-cast, and the caster has to supplement this lack of line weight by extra muscular effort. If the line is too heavy, then it pulls the rod tip back too easily, the rod feels soggy and without spring. The line falls easily to the ground and it will not 'hold up'.

It is obvious why we have to share an internationally agreed code of line weights, so that no matter what type of rod we own, we can buy a matching line for it, anywhere in the world. And since lines are made of different materials to give particular performances (i.e. floating, sinking etc), then the code applies to the weights of all these lines. The code, known as the A.F.T.M. scale, is based on the weight in grains of the first 30 ft. of the fly line, which is that part of the line doing most of the work.

Since its introduction, this system has worked efficiently, in spite of slight manufacturing differences and the fact that the tip of a fly line, before the taper begins, has to be excluded from the code. It means, for example, that if a rod is flexed nicely by 30 ft. of fly line weighing 160 grains, then the line size for that rod is 6. 185 grains gives us a size 7, and 210 a size 8. We don't need to know this, for modern practice is to mark the correct line loading on the butt of the rod.

The boon of this system is that no matter what line we choose, from fast sinker to floater, from a double-taper to a torpedo-head, if we choose the right size it will make the rod flex perfectly.

The first fly lines were made of braided horsehair, and such a line would have been used by Izaak Walton and his contemporary Sir Henry Cotton, who contributed a section on fly-fishing to *The Compleat Angler*. Then silk was woven into the hair, until late in the nineteenth century the first oil-dressed silk lines appeared, as fished by Viscount Grey, F. M. Halford, Skues and others of that era. The post-war years introduced first nylon-cored lines, where the taper was in the plastic coating and not in the core as it was with the old silk lines. This was followed by the use of heavier synthetic fibres, such as Dacron, for sinking fly lines. Then silk lines were given a new lease of life by siliconising the surface, so that today we can buy from a whole range of materials to give a wide tactical choice, from floating lines to those that sink at different speeds, and finally the anti-skate lines, the tips of which sink though the main belly still floats.

The normal double-taper fly line has a profile similar to a pair of rats' tails joined together at their roots. The more the line is extended, the more weight pulls at the rod tip, and casting grows easier. Yet, at the same time, the line moving through the rod-rings gets thicker as more line is extended, thus slowing down the shoot by increased friction. This is one reason for compressing the weight of the line into a relatively short belly, which is quickly worked outside of the rod, and behind which is a finer, shooting line.

Modern fly-line profiles:
above,
double-tapered line; *below,*
forward taper

Such a fly line, in a single unit, has various names: Forward Taper, Torpedo Head, Rocket Taper, and so forth. We are already moving towards a casting projectile, such as the made-up shooting head, which is a Forward-Taper fly line in an exaggerated form. These various profiles and performances were also written into the A.F.T.M. code. For example, a size 6 weight-forward floating line would be coded WF6F, which is self-explanatory. A size 8 sinking double-taper line is simply DT8S.

The choice of line performance is invariably dictated by tactics. Dry-fly fishing, upstream nymph, surface fishing on still water, these all indicate a floating line. Deep work in cold water for spring salmon, searching the bed of a lake, avoiding skate on a torrential river, these cry out for a sinking line. The choice of profile is altogether different. The distance caster prefers the weight-forward line because the resistance to line-shoot is vastly reduced, and all the casting weight is quickly worked out into the air. Dry-fly and nymph specialists may prefer double-taper lines because they can be put down on the water with far more finesse, while salmon anglers can roll-cast them off the water when high banks behind impede the normal overhead cast.

Certain features of modern plastic lines haven't been terribly satisfactory. For instance, the tips of plastic lines were often too thick to turn over the nylon leader at the last gasp of a long cast, and the forward-taper lines should have had relatively short bellies with a fine-diameter shooting line behind. These two features were incorporated into the 'Fast Taper' fly lines, made specially for me.

Nor is it certain that white fly lines are the least visible, if only for the reason that such lines always seem to catch the sun. I have always preferred dull pastel shades, especially for the floating lines, and while we must have a polished surface for good shooting, at least we should keep this to a necessary minimum.

Shooting Heads

I doubt if there's more confusion on any other aspect of fly-fishing than shooting heads. Too many articles have been written with too little experimental bases for them.

Shooting heads are exaggerated forms of the weight-forward fly line. The weight of the head conforms to the belly of the fly line which pulls against the rod tip, helping to wind it up like a spring. The head is cut from the end of a double taper line and the butt is then joined to a fine nylon monofilament of a diameter from 40/100 to 45/100 mm. Because this nylon is much finer than a normal fly line, there's far less resistance through the rod rings during the casting routine, and hence the shoot can be prodigious.

It has been said that the length and weight of the shooting head isn't critical. This is absolutely wrong. The loading has to be far more precise than with the normal fly line simply because you cannot introduce more weight into the cast by extending more line. It becomes apparent that the head itself is a weight/length ratio, the weight being sufficient to flex the rod within a length of line which can be held comfortably in the air. Such a length normally works out between 30–36 ft. To compress enough casting weight within such a comfortable length it is necessary to cut the shooting head from a fly line one or two sizes more than that normally recommended for the rod.

But this is academic. You just cannot gamble with a new fly line. It you cut it too short, then the rod will be underpowered, and one thing you can't easily do is to put back the surplus line-belly you've already cut off. On the other hand, if the head is too long, and by the same token, overweight, then you can never get a good turnover of the leader. It lands all in a heap. Remember the rod is casting a static, fixed weight in the shooting head, which must be precisely correct.

The way to work this out is to run a double taper fly line onto the reel, one or two sizes more than the normal loading, and to make two marks with white paint at 30 and 36 ft. from the tip of the line. Now, in some convenient space, extend the line by false casting until you aerialise enough line to flex the rod, which is, at the same time, a comfortable and manageable length in the air. It should fall between the two marks at the rod tip. Be sure to do this false casting in different directions of wind, for with the wind in front of you the line will not pull backwards unless it is heavy enough.

When you are satisfied, cut the line at the tip ring, and this makes your shooting head. The butt-end may be spliced permanently to the shooting line, but I prefer to make small loops to the tips and butts of my line in cellulose varnish thinners, stripping away the plastic coat from the braided core along this short length and whipping back the core on to itself with button thread to make a neat loop. The whipping is varnished. Shooting heads of various types can be made up in this way, floating, sinking at various speeds, sink-tips. They are interchangeable on the same reel-drum on which lies the shooting nylon line, and joined when required by a tidy tucked blood-knot. These heads occupy little room in the tackle bag, and as it takes some short while for the shooting line to become free from coil and cling, interchangeability of heads to suit different fishing tactics is economic in time as well as in space.

If you have access to an accurate balance, once you have a 'master' head, you can weigh any type of fly line against it, cutting back, say from 40 ft., until the pans equalise, or you can simply weigh out the new head from a known weight in grains or grammes.

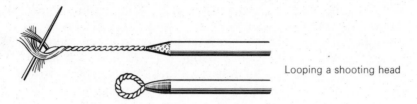

Looping a shooting head

Remember that if you scale up shooting head and fly rod combinations you eventually reach a point when the outfit is uncontrollable, the head whipping back so fiercely as to destroy turnover and crack off the fly. Start with a lightish fly rod, normal fly line loading of which is size 6, and make your heads from size 7 lines, or at most size 8.

The nylon shooting line can be of almost any regular nylon. A specially flattened nylon may give more freedom from tangle, but less distance due to the increased friction area of line against rod ring. Personally I use a special soft and fine nylon from France called 'Nylorfi'.

Fly Reels

Fly reels have always been considered unimportant, which explains why their design remained unchanged for so long. Since a fly rod casts well with no reel at all, it is obvious that the traditional idea of the reel balancing the rod is wrong, and it follows from this that the best reel is the lightest one to hold the line and backing.

There are many efficient, single-speed fly reels on the market, the guide to sensible choice being a robust construction and flash-free finish. If the drum is uncaged so that you can exert finger pressure on it, so much the better. Beware of sharp pillars which remove the surface from a fly line. These are all matters of commonsense, but is it worth paying more for sophistication?

The geared fly reels are a great improvement on the single-speed models for still-water fishing, but what it boils down to is this: of the two ways of playing fish, the old way of controlling line through the fingers created the idea that the reel was comparatively unimportant. In recent years two things have changed this view, firstly that the average weight of trout has increased, due to new methods of stocking and raising fish, and secondly that we are all casting much further, particularly on lakes. Therefore when a fish is hooked there's usually spare line around our feet, spare line which should be whipped back on to the drum as quickly as possible.

We will come to the playing of fish later, but for now it suffices to say that most modern fly fishermen prefer to play from the reel, and the faster and earlier loose line can be retrieved the safer will be the act of playing out the fish. This has caused a welcome change in reel design, and indeed it has promoted the fly reel to the rank of being an important item in our equipment.

A fine brown trout caught by national casting champion Barry Welham with an automatic fly reel

The ultimate in fast line retrieve is the automatic fly reel whereby the line can literally be zipped back on to the drum by pressing a lever. Although this makes sense as a first impression, and although a small number of anglers grow to love these reels, to me automatics are ruled out by a number of drawbacks, not least the fact that they are uncomfortably heavy. On three occasions I've seen a skilled man lose fish, for just as the line was zipped tight, the rainbow skied himself, tearing the hook away from the jaw. It happened twice running to a friend, who swore he would forsake such mechanical aids for the rest of his fishing life. You may get used to an automatic fly reel, but it may have already cost you the fish of a lifetime.

My choice is for a geared fly reel with dull finish and of little weight, with external flange to the drum for finger control. The Shakespeare 'Speedex' reel is the best I have yet used.

Leaders

The leader is the invisible link between the fly line and the fly. It can be made from a level length of nylon, but since it has to be turned over by the impetus of the fly-line to straighten and deliver the fly accurately and with finesse, it is better to use tapered leaders. We visualise this as a continuous taper from the line belly, right on through the leader to the fly so that the energy of the cast can be smoothly transmitted.

Considering the number of jobs the leader has to perform, its structure has to be worked out with some precision. Let me recapitulate these factors:

1. The leader must transmit the energy of the cast.
2. It must present the fly in such a way as to avoid alarming the fish, either in its appearance or in the way in which it falls on the water.
3. It must hold the fly so that it works properly.
4. It must be strong enough to master the fight of the quarry without rupture.

The leader must be a combination of various qualities to achieve these purposes, sometimes in varying conditions, as for example the difference between a short storm leader to be pushed into the teeth of a near-gale and, at the other extreme, the long, fine leader for surface fishing in calm, bright conditions when even the finest nylon stands out on the water like a hawser.

The transmission of energy depends on the leader being correctly balanced to the fly line at one end and the fly at the other. Fly line tips are usually about 0·030 in. in diameter. If the step down from line tip to leader butt is greater than one third in diameter, then the line cannot grab hold of the leader and turn it over. Instead the leader and fly fall in a big heap at the last gasp of the cast. Obviously the minimum diameter of the leader's butt must be 0·020 in. or approximately 28 lb. breaking strain in regular nylon.

It's difficult to scale down a leader in sections from 28 lbs. b.s. to, say, 6 lb. at the point, which is why I insisted on finer tips for my own 'Fast Taper' fly-lines.

The joining together of nylon sections for leaders is by means of knots, shown later. Here we're concerned with the balance of the leader. Visualising the whole leader as comprising of three sections, the thick butt, the middle section and finally the point to which the fly is attached, the proportions are as follows: butt – 60%; middle segment – 20%; point – 20%. This could be a simple, tapered leader made from three lengths of nylon, but as the step-down between the diameters might be too great, especially if a fine point is needed for smaller flies, then each section could be sub-divided into two, giving a continuous taper from butt to point of six lengths of nylon.

For making leaders to this simple formula, some data is needed. We need to know the diameter of the point of the fly line, and since I've never known any manufacturer to record this, a micrometer would be most useful. Next, we need to employ the same brand of nylon throughout the leader since its reduction would be uniform. Enthusiasts may keep 25-yard spools mounted on a rod, with a steel measure nearby. Finally, we need to know the length of the leader required and the diameter of its point, so that the step-down can be worked out. The point-diameter is determined by the size of flies or lures to be used, because a thick nylon can't go through the eye of a tiny fly, while fine nylon will hinge weakly on a big lure, eventually losing it because of fatigue of the material.

Here are two tables, one of diameters of a regular nylon in relation to its breaking strain. You can easily make up a similar table for your own favourite brand. The other table shows approximate safe nylon points for given fly sizes.

Old Gut Class (Plate Gauge)	Diameter Metric	Diameter Inches, 1000	Approx. Breaking Strain
1/5	50/100	·021	32 lb
2/5	48/100	·020	28 lb
3/5	45/100	·019	26 lb
4/5	43/100	·018	24 lb
5/5	40/100	·017	20 lb
6/5	28/100	·016	18 lb
7/5	35/100	·015	16 lb
8/5	32/100	·014	14 lb
9/5	30/100	·013	12·0 lb
10/5	28/100	·012	11·0 lb
0X	26/100	·011	9·0 lb
1X	24/100	·010	8·0 lb
2X	22/100	·009	7·0 lb
3X	18/100	·008	6·0 lb
4X	16/100	·007	4·0 lb
5X	15/100	·006	3·0 lb
6X	14/100	·005	2·0 lb

Point Size	Fly Size, Redditch Scale
0X	1/0 – 2
1X	4 – 8
2X	6 – 10
3X	10 – 14
4X	12 – 16
5X	14 – 18
6X	16 – 20

These proportions conform to our first factor of transmitting the energy of the cast to the leader and fly. They also go some of the way to satisfying the second factor of finesse in presentation, but two more things need to be done:

Nylon glitters in sunlight. For dry-fly and nymph fishing just below the surface this glitter has to be removed. Before the nylon is knotted together, rub it down gently with a fine abrasive powder in a piece of cloth, moistened slightly. I find 'Vim' to work well. You take off the surface shine and the nylon turns a dull grey. Its transparency is gone, but this doesn't matter so long as the shine has been removed.

Until it absorbs some water, nylon is stiff. We need to condition the leaders so that they straighten from the first cast, cutting easily through the surface film. After many trials, including the use of hot water and small weights, I've hit on a foolproof way of conditioning leaders. It's simply to store them overnight, before the fishing trip, between leaves of felt moistened in a 10% glycerine and water mixture. This softens the nylon beautifully, so that you're ready to take a fish from the first cast of the day rather than to wait for a fretful half-hour for the nylon to rid itself of springiness.

The science of making leaders can be taken to amazing complexity. We can make a double-taper leader for distance casting by tying in a thicker nylon belly in a section of the leader, two thirds of its length from the point. I dwell here on basic needs.

A short leader is one of 7½ ft. Its purpose is for punching a lure into the teeth of a strong wind. You cannot present a small fly delicately on a short leader, and the normal length for average conditions is 9 ft. Extra long leaders beyond this length are used for delicate dry fly and nymph presentation in light airs, very bright, calm conditions when small flies are the rule. Remember that when joining nylon sections with normal blood knots, it's not safe to reduce diameters by more than ·002 in. at a time (roughly 2 lb. b.s.), or the knot may slip.

Let's take an example for making up a normal leader to a 6-lb. point for a fly line with a tip diameter of ·025 in. The butt section is 42 in. of 0·018 in. nylon, joined to 30 in. of 0·016 in. and then to three sections, each of 6 in. of 0·014 in., 0·012 in. and 0·010 in. Finally, tie in the point of 18 in. of 0·008 in., which is 6 lb. b.s.

With practice, you can work out from the tables your leader lengths for different tasks and your final point diameters to suit the size of fly, then proportion these to butt, middle section and point before cutting and knotting together.

As to accessories, most are dictated by commonsense. For example, normal fly line backing should be a braided polyester because nylon mono-filament would compress the drum, distorting or even breaking it. Backing is used to fill the drum of the reel and to provide extra yardage for the big catch when it runs hard for the deep-green yonder.

The nets, cast-carriers, fly-boxes, priest for braining trout and salmon, all change frequently in design and you will have to make your own choice from what is available. But be sure to pay considerable attention to one other vital item of equipment, the waders. They are important because if you lose your foothold in a fast current you can easily drown. I have never liked the traditional hob-nailed wader because when the studs are slightly worn they become slippery, especially on weed-covered rocks, while their weight is inconvenient and the grating noise between metal and gravel scares every fish for yards.

Modern wader design offers a slip-proof sole, much like the tread of a racing-car tyre. The tread is shaped to resist the pressure of the current when the boot is clamped to a dangerous surface. These boots are fairly light, tight at the ankle to prevent the foot slopping about inside, and they clip down below the knee for walking. My own favourite wader, which I have used from reservoir silt to rocky salmon river, is called the 'Griplastic', made in France by the firm of Hutchinson.

The Fly Hook

If you read fly fishing books and articles over a long period of time, one item of equipment is consistently denigrated, the fly hook. Recently, a well-known fly-tyer claimed that 80% of his hooks broke in the vice or when fishing. I've never been convinced that fly hooks were as bad as that! Yet there are problems. Taking hooks as a whole, we have seen a growing tradition for buying cheap hooks from abroad, the reason for which is the insistence by the angler that the fly should cost little. While fly prices in other countries doubled, or even trebled, due to increased costs for materials and skilled labour, the British angler still had, and even now has his 'shilling fly'. The hook quality was one of the things that had to be reduced. The reputation of firms making good quality hooks suffered because they were known here for their commercial qualities, the cheap, mass-market hook.

A rainbow that didn't escape from the new Bucknall-designed fly hook

I've never known why manufacturers lacked the courage to advance fly prices, but gradually the old fly-tying rooms were closed down, and much of the indigenous manufacture replaced by importation from the Orient, while at home, the angler swung over to making his own flies. This again drove to the surface the need for high-quality fly hooks, and while they were rarely used in commercial production, patterns like the Partridge Wide-Gape served amateur tyers well.

The shortcoming of cheap fly hooks lies not so much in their quality but in certain aspects of their design. For example, we all experience fish which take boldly but which soon shed the hook. Sometimes this is due to the angle of strike being too acute, or the hook skidding off hard tissue in the mouth of the fish, but too often the hook failed to penetrate, a factor enhanced by the glass rods with their lighter tips. I discussed this with other anglers, among them Britain's Richard Walker, and it seemed that the problem was that barbs are cut too deeply. Taking several patterns at random, under a low-powered microscope barbs were not cut below 15% of the depth of the wire, and often the cut was far deeper, giving quite a rank barb.

I took this problem to the French fish-hook maker, Viellard-Migeon (V.M.C.), who until then did not have a fly hook in their range. This gave Christophe Viellard the chance to make an entirely new pattern of trout hook from scratch, and I asked if I might design it for him. I was invited to the factory at Morvillars and was soon in discussion with the technicians. You must bear in mind that the new hook had to be made within the limitations of modern, mechanised production, where wire goes into one side of a huge machine and completed hooks tumble out the other side, to await the final polishing, tempering and bronzing. This is the list of features I wanted in the new fly hook:

1. Short point for quick penetration, especially with the modern, light-tipped glass rods often striking at long range.
2. Short barb cut at a depth of no more than 10% of the metal to eliminate point-breakage on the strike, and poor penetration.
3. Round-bend to eliminate any pointed or uneven stress-places, as in the Limerick shape, for instance.
4. A 'cut point' instead of the old-fashioned ground points, which, being rounded like a needle, can only puncture the skin. The 'Cut Point' has a sabre-like cutting edge for surer penetration on the strike.
5. A wide-gape which keeps the shank well away from the point in striking, avoiding the glance blow which skates the hook point along, rather than into the mouth tissue of the fish. It also gives better hooking powers and posture for the hackled dry fly.
6. A straight shank which doesn't weaken or distort when compressed in the fly-tyers' vices, a danger of 'offset' patterns.
7. The elimination of all grinding processes in the hook manufacture, which weakens the shank where metal is taken away, and which, by heating the metal by friction prematurely, makes it impossible to obtain a uniform tempering of the hook.
8. The 'forging' of the bend and shank for extra strength. 'Forging' actually

means the squaring and compressing of the wire in chosen places, a process which considerably strengthens the hook.

All these qualities were admirably achieved in the prototypes by the technicians of V.M.C. The biggest headache was my insistence about the elimination of grinding, for the normal habit in fly hook manufacture is to diminish the eye by tapering the metal before it is turned over to form the small loop. In the end, I hit on the idea of forging the metal just before the loop to give the eye a 'square-to-square' finish. We did wind up with a slightly larger eye than on traditional hooks, which may be appreciated by those who need to fish very small flies to larger trout, requiring stronger nylon points. It also makes it easier for those tying on flies with poor eyesight or in failing light. I was prepared to accept the larger eye to avoid danger from the hook, the temper of which would be uneven because of metal being ground away.

All this care on design paid off. Not long after development of the prototype was complete I caught three rainbow trout over $4\frac{1}{2}$ lb., one being 6 lb. 2 oz., while thanks to better penetration of the hook on the strike few, if any, 'takes' were lost.

Line retrieve, pinching the line against the butt with the right hand in case of sudden take

3   Knots

The first thing that needs to be said about knots is that there are far more than one has uses for them. The best idea is to discover a reliable knot for a particular purpose and stick to it. The second thing is that when nylon monofilament and plastic-coated fly lines were introduced, an entire generation of knots based on silk and gut became obsolete.

The way to learn any knot is to tie it a few times with a thick cord. The efficiency of all our knots is destroyed by pulling them tight too quickly. Finer nylons especially will kink or guillotine themselves, while the turns of complex knots will not bed down evenly. Knots should be tightened steadily and slowly.

Fly fishermen need three types of knot – the loop for the end of a leader, that used to tie on a fly and that for joining two lengths of nylon, usually of different diameters. Here are a number of knots I've personally found reliable, though it goes without saying that any knot must weaken the tackle system by at least 10%, sometimes more.

Perfection Loop

This knot forms the loop in nylon, say for the end of a leader, and is easily tied by following the line-drawing. It has the twin virtues of keeping the loop in line with the leader, while the bulk of the knot is quite small.

Perfection leader end loop

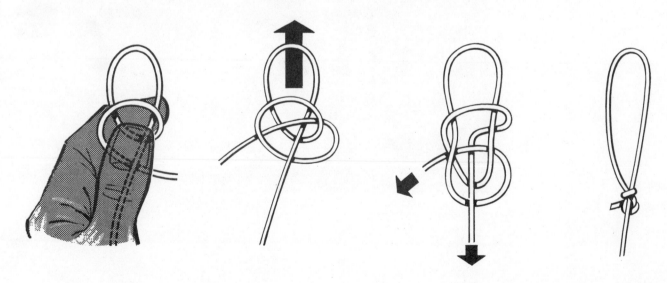

48

Blood Loop

Although this knot is bulkier than the Perfection, it is also stronger. It also keeps the knot in a straight line in relation to the leader and, as the diagram shows, is both quick and easy to tie.

Blood loop

Blood Knot

This knot is the safest for joining together two lengths of nylon where the diameters do not differ by more than 0·015 in., or, say, 2 lb. in breaking strain.

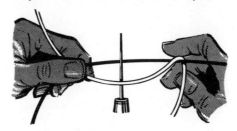

Blood knot

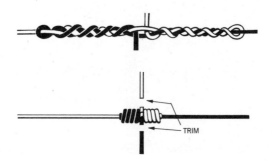

TRIM

I find it easier to tie this knot at the bench by having a needle to keep the central loop open until the two ends can be pushed through. The knot should be tied with the nylon quite dry and the coils gently snuggled down with the thumbnails as the knot is tightened. I also leave the slightest fraction of a tail on the trimmed ends to allow for bedding down.

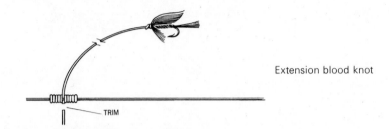

Extension blood knot

Some say that it's unsafe to leave one of the tails uncut, to attach a dropper, but if the fly is tied to the higher strand of nylon, then the fish cannot escape, even if the knot gives. In fishing, though, I have never experienced this knot failing when the stronger strand is used for the dropper fly.

Overhand knot

Stu Apte Knot

This variation of the blood knot, invented by a well known American angler, is intended to balance up the weaker side of a blood knot when it's necessary to join together two strands of nylon of widely differing diameters, as for example, when making a steeply-tapered 'storm' leader to punch into strong winds. It is simply a normal blood knot, the finer nylon of which has been doubled. It is most useful by the water's edge, when time precludes making a more complicated, secure knot like the double nail.

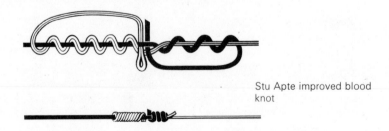

Stu Apte improved blood knot

Tucked Blood-knot

After many trials and tribulations, this is the only knot I rely on for tying a fly to the leader. It is quite safe, provided that the end is tucked back through the loop, as shown, and it's easy and quick to tie while fishing.

Unlike the Turle, which was safe enough in the days of gut casts but which I find unreliable with nylon, it allows the fly to hinge freely, to find its own posture on the water and to move freely in the current below the surface.

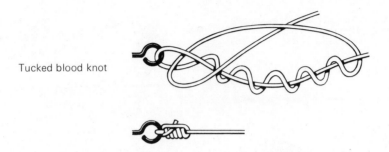

Tucked blood knot

The Nail Knot

This knot is excellent for attaching the nylon leader to the end of a plastic-coated fly line, though it will quickly slice through silk lines. A variation of this knot is popular, whereby the nylon is first taken through the core of the fly line, to centralise it, and the tip of the line then streamlined with varnished whipping thread. This isn't practical, though, with the modern, finer-tipped fly lines described earlier. As the tips of the 'Fast Taper' fly lines are very fine, the lack of centralising the knot is unimportant.

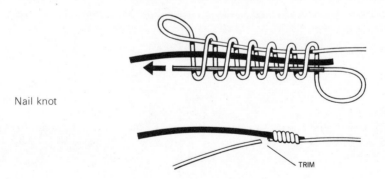

Nail knot

TRIM

The drawing clearly shows how the knot is formed. It takes its name from a nail, used to keep the coils open while the end is passed back through them, a task facilitated by using a small piece of plastic or metal tube, which can be slipped off the end of the line, leaving it in situ. As the knot is tightened it bites into the tough plastic coating, gaining a secure hold. It is not bulky and slips through the end ring of the fly rod with a slight 'tick'.

Double Nail Knot

This knot, best tied at home, is valuable for making steeply-tapered leaders of strong material, say for salmon fishing. Two separate nail knots are made, then slid together and tightened. It's quite possible and safe to join nylons differing in breaking strains by as much as 5 lb.

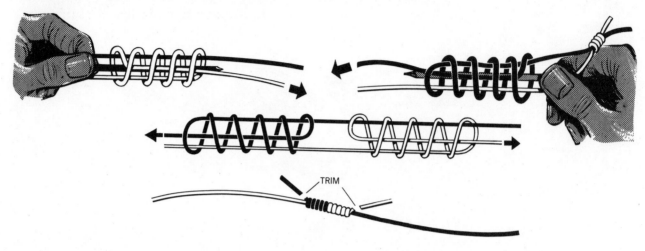

Double nail knot

Offset Nail Knot

Finally in this family of nail knots we come to that quite rare occasion when we have to join a nylon to a material of considerably greater thickness, and we need to add a safety margin. To do this, the thicker material forms a two-turn nail knot over the finer end, and this is tightened down somewhat while the normal nail knot is formed 'on the other side'. The two halves are then snugged against each other in the usual way and tightened fully. This even allows sections with differences of 10 lb. b.s. to be joined together.

Offset nail knot

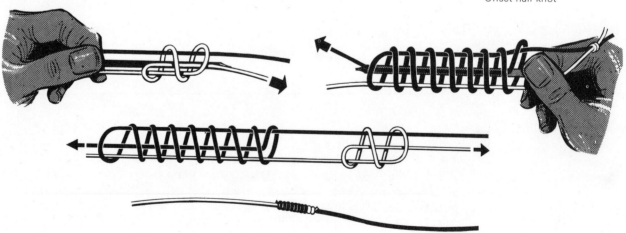

4   Striking and Playing

Striking simply means setting the hook firmly in the jaw of the fish. More fish are lost at this vital time than at any other. It happens that we occasionally lose fish in playing, sometimes just as we exert the final leverage to pull the fish over the rim of the net, but it doesn't happen often. On the other hand, every fly fisherman would admit to losing many fish on the 'take'. The annoying thing is that it seems to happen in cycles, some days fish after fish coming unstuck.

With the single-handed trout rod, the strike has to be much firmer than in days gone by, because modern glass rods have much lighter tips than the old cane rods. The traditional advice for a strike when dry fly fishing was to pause, then flick upward with the wrist. The time when I missed most fish was when I converted to glass but continued to strike as if I had a cane rod in the hand. My dry-fly work has been confined to chalk streams and smaller, fairly slow streams in the Weald of Kent. In recent times, when fishing for brownies on the River Eaulne in Normandy, I missed two good rises because of this 'pause'. This river was much faster in flow, the trout were used to seizing flies quickly, and rejecting unpalatable things just as fast. I speeded up my striking, giving a firm, upward lift of the whole forearm, and thereafter hooked every fish.

The dry fly is good for novices because when they stalk a rising fish they have time to cool themselves down before they cast. The position of the fish is marked in relation to, say, a plant or bush on the bank, and the rise can be expected as the fly floats over that mark. When the fish takes the fly, then hand and rod react together, in slowish streams affording a slight pause to pull the hook home against the diving fish, but in faster water enabling you to strike quickly.

Experience is the only guide to making allowance for the cushioning effect of the rod's flex and the elasticity of the nylon leader (which is one reason I shortened points and barbs on my fly hook design). Everyone must lose a few fish to learn how to make the necessary adjustments between too weak a blow and too powerful a reaction. The only thing in favour of the upstream dry-fly is that the fly must be pulled into the fish, whereas in downstream wet-fly fishing the strike may well pull the fly right out of the trout's mouth.

53

Wet-fly fishing downstream is both the easiest and most difficult of techniques, and the margin between average performer and expert are wide. It is easy in the sense that the current straightens out poorly cast lines. In practice the 'take' is often sudden and unexpected, the fish being either 'on' or 'off' before the angler can react. The expert, though, is always in touch with his fly as it swings across the current, with the line having enough belly to act as a striking spring. He knows where and when the fish may hit the fly, so that the rod and line are ready to respond. It's a trick that comes through fishing, not through books. If it's any comfort, the rod-line-fly relationship for striking is the same as for fishing the wet fly well, without too big a belly as the fly swings round, and without the rod-tip being too far away from the line, in either its leading or following position.

Now let's consider the actual holding of the line for striking an anticipated 'take'. Both in river and lake fishing, the left hand has to draw line to fish the flies at a chosen speed and depth, as well as to retrieve them for the next cast. The forefinger of my right hand pinches the line against the rod-butt above the reel, easing off pressure as the left hand retrieves, squeezing it against the butt again as the left hand releases the line for another pull. This way the line can be held tightly against any 'take', no matter when it happens.

In stream fishing, the hardest striking is with the upstream nymph, even though the fly is being pulled into the fish, and not away from it when fishing down a river. The problems are twofold, first in the actual sight of the 'take' and secondly in keeping the line tight enough for the fly to fish naturally without skidding the leader on the surface.

As for the first, no matter how often it's described, knowing when a trout takes the nymph is largely a matter of instinct. Sometimes the leader will check in its flow back with the current, as if a leaf has stopped the fly. It may pull down through an invisible hole. You may see a wink of light as a fish turns onto the fly, or a patch of white, being the triangle of the lower jaw opening to accept your offering. You cannot strike too quickly at these signs.

In clear water, or when the fish are chopping off nymphs as they come up to hatch, there's no real problem, for here it's like the dry fly, with the same type of boil to the fly showing on the surface. The nymph, though, is the ideal way of searching water above you when fish aren't rising, or when it's too coloured to spot trout. One stream I fish is almost always stained with some mud and iron. It is never free from some colour, and I have learned to pitch the nymph to likely spots where no fish is seen. I must read the signs, strike them to succeed, and the more I do, the more successful I am. In one evening session I caught trout I never saw, striking by instinct as it were.

When I first started salmon fishing I was confused by the contradictory advice on striking. One advocated method frightened me with its risk of failure. This was to throw a large loop of line downstream when the fish took the fly, to let the current take the iron into the side of the salmon's mouth. I've never had the courage to attempt this, but I did evolve a method which hasn't failed me for those slow, firm takes when the fish chases the fly from its lie, then returns to it. I raise the rod and squeeze the line firmly against the butt, allowing the fish to pull the hook into its jaw as it makes its way back across the current. In sub-surface summer fishing with light, low water flies, I usually hit them as I would a large trout on the wet fly.

Striking on Still-water

For the majority of fly fishermen, still-water trout present the greatest striking problem. In dry-fly work we know which way the trout is facing, we see it take the fly and we pull the hook into the fish, against its body weight. In still water the fish can approach the fly, often unseen, through a circle of 360 degrees, and the hard fact is that we must accept a proportion of badly struck fish where the hook is being pulled in the same direction as the fish is moving, which leads to that glancing blow, with the hook point skimming off the cartilagenous tissue of the jaw. In such a typical miss, the fish is felt briefly to wiggle, then comes unstuck. Also, whereas we often cast to a visible trout, frequently we fish the water and the 'take' may come with sudden surprise, followed by our own too hurried, or too late response.

Our response is a matter of concentration, for the habitual still-water angler knows when his chances are heightened, when activity of insects, birds over the water or rising fish key his interest. The strike, generally on lakes, though, should be upright and firm, with a longish sweep of the arm to counter-act the elasticity of the tackle system.

Another problem is due to the larger lures on big hooks, which when hit by small fish fail to penetrate because the strike merely pulls the fish through the water as its weight is insufficient to act as a striking block.

The great discovery in fighting a fish was made by Alexander Wanless who used to catch huge salmon on his 'threadlines' of very low breaking strain. He asserted that fish fought against pressure, that if the pressure were eased as soon as the fish was hooked, the angler could move to an advantageous position while his opponent returned passively to its lie, and then, by gentle pressure it could be beaten. I found this worked with big pike, and, later, with large trout.

This is true to some extent when playing any fish, and the 'feel' which develops is based on it, with the sub-conscious knowledge of the critical moment when to ease pressure.

Translated into actuality, I have hooked a strong four-pound rainbow on a lake. At the start, I know the probability of it being a rainbow trout, either from the stocking policy of the fishery or simply because I saw the fish before casting to it, or during the first movement of the trout against the strike caught a glimpse of the magenta band on its flank. I immediately know the weight of the fish by its first rush, and I know from experience of playing rainbows that it will almost certainly leap through the surface or flurry on top of the water, both dangerous moments.

The aim is obvious: to tire the fish until it can be coaxed to the net. You must put on fairly strong pressure, keeping the rod reasonably high to absorb any sudden shocks or lunges. Having some slack line in hand, you must also be prepared to let this slip when the fish makes one of its sizzling runs. The leap and flurry can be anticipated, for it's usually the result of the fish dashing

The dangerous moment is
when a strong fish flurries on
the surface on a tight line . . .

away under pressure and being forced upward to the surface. The response to this is to ease off line pressure on the fish, and if it does throw itself high into the air then lay the rod over to prevent the full weight of the trout being thrown against a tight, relatively weak link, the point of the leader.

The sad truth is that when beginners start fly fishing they learn to play fish successfully by losing quite a number. As we've already noted, words are a pale substitute for experience. By trial and error you learn all the subtle adaptations and adjustments needed in casting, striking and playing a fish in different situations. One day you might find yourself playing out a strong lake specimen in a wide area, perhaps a quarry, which fights with little strategy, rarely bolting for sanctuary in snags, roots or the like, as would a hefty chub in a small unkempt stream. Another day you may have to deal with a powerful trout in the confines of a river, such as the Test, where weed-

'I lay the rod over to prevent the full weight of the trout being thrown against a tight leader . . .'

A trout comes to the net

beds and weirs abound. You can hardly allow the fish to make long, powerful runs against firm pressure, especially as the dry fly leader will be of gossamer nylon.

I well remember shooting for a big brown trout lying between weed-beds just a few yards from a tumbling weir, on the River Test. It was bright sunlight, forcing me to use a leader the point of which was only 2 lb. in breaking strain. The trout was leisurely knocking off Pale Wateries, the tiniest of light-coloured floating flies. My copy of it he took without criticism. I flicked the hook home, and threw him a slack line. The fish circled, bemusedly, then returned to its original position in classical Wanless style. I had cast up from behind his tail, so my presence was unknown. I lay flat on the bank, net well sunk, then tightening the line enough to take in the slack eased the big fish back under very gentle rod pressure. The weir run pulled it back a little faster and at the vital moment he came over the hidden net, so my one 'shot' at him was a successful scoop.

Two strong fish, one in a wide open lake, the other imprisoned within river banks, yet each as strong as the other, and both had to be brought safely to net. The lake trout was encouraged to tire himself out against strong rod pressure, eased off only to cushion dangerous shocks. The river trout had to be coaxed into the net, virtually without realising anything was amiss. If such things can be taught only by experience, at least advice can give one guide. Most fly fishermen tackle the immediate problem, that of striking the fish, without thought of how to handle the hooked opponent until its first frightened lunge is felt. It takes only a moment of thought to decide in what way a fish hooked in a certain place should be brought safely to the net.

Such a habit would be worth far more than the usual recitation of habits of various species when hooked – that rainbows and sea-trout leap, that brown-trout bore deeply, that grilse make long, powerful runs, that grayling play sideways across the stream, giving their large dorsal fin full play. These generalisations are valid only insofar as all generalisations are true, and prone to exceptions, while they cannot excuse failure to plan the capture of the fish from the cast to the final, despairing flip over the edge of the net.

5　The Fly

Could you imagine golf where you had a choice of many different sizes of golf ball for each shot, and perhaps you had made these balls yourself the week before? Horrifying, isn't it, that we've ploughed through the casting sequences, the tackle considerations, and here we are, up tight against all types and condition of fly? No better time is there to remind ourselves that the fish is a creature low down in the order of things, whose reaction to the surrounding world is instinctive. In the case of protected lake and stream fisheries, the bulk of fish have been grown artificially like battery hens and most of them will be killed within a short time of their introduction into the fishery. Their reaction to the artificial fly may even happen before they have adapted to the idea of finding natural food, for their previous experience of Man and food was that the one threw in the other.

We do not make the fly complex because the fish is intelligent. On the contrary, it is a subtle way of writing conservation into the sport because of the stupidity of the fish. It is also encouraging to know that a trout, for example, will frequently respond to the movement of almost any fly, and that its presentation is of far more importance than its colour, shape and size.

It's true that, on certain fisheries, the fly becomes important because the rules make it so; for example, the dry-fly rule. Yet the vast majority of lakes, rivers and reservoirs leave you free to choose whatever type of fly you prefer. Artificial flies are related to the feeding behaviour of fish, and while some experts have surmised on many feeding patterns, provocation, competition, aggression and others, we can simplify it into two.

Let's call the first of these the 'random' response. This happens when food is scarce and fish are hungry. The obvious time is in the early season. The water is cold, insect and crustacea are dormant and protected by Nature against the trout because of its habit of recognising its food by a form of activity, such as hatching, egg-laying and so forth. Trout could literally starve over unmoving fauna at this time of year, and stomachs are often found to be empty in waters the bottoms of which are known to harbour myriads of live creatures who will spring to life when the fishery warms up.

At such times and places the trout roam widely, ready to pounce on anything that moves. One fish I took was full of catkins that had wriggled attractively as they fell into the lake from overhanging branches. These fish are easy to catch on almost any type of fly, and it accounts for the massacres of trout reported from lakes and reservoirs when they first open in a cold spring.

The second feeding behaviour we can term 'preoccupied'. It's caused by a prolific form of activity at a given time. Examples are numerous, the hatch of the Lake Olive in a bay, the collecting of dense crowds of small fry around weed fronds in September, the fall of the spent female Mayfly spinners after egg-laying. The fish become programmed to the size, type, colour and activity of the prey they are taking repetitiously, and imitative fly fishing has to be practised correctly for chance of success.

If we broke down all artificial flies and lures into two groups we could fit them into one of these behaviour patterns. Most lures, for example, provoke the random predatory response, except when a closer small-fish imitation is put to a trout seen to be harrowing fry. Most dry flies are cast during the hatch of the insects they copy, except when, for example, a general pattern provokes an idly resting fish. We make rules for easier comprehension, but we delight in exceptions and paradoxes.

And when we read descriptions of flies, the writer will tell us immediately if the pattern deliberately copies a known form of food, or whether it is a general attractor pattern. The trouble is that there are no clear divisions of flies, the one merges into the other, and on the borderland are general flies which serve both purposes, though to deal with them will only confuse us now. We see, too, how a flashy lure can serve different purposes at different times, sometimes exciting the random feeder, sometimes imitating the small fish.

We also divide flies according to their physical behaviour in or on the water. The dry fly is, of course, the fly which floats, the rest are 'wet flies', though strictly speaking these may also be nymphs or lures. Traditionally, flies have been made from scraps of fur, silk and feather tied to the hook shank, but in recent years we have introduced tinsels and plastics into their make-up.

We choose materials for our flies according to the prescriptions laid down in manuals from their inventors. This defines the colour and the way in which the stuff is fixed to the hook shank. It also decides the way the fly will behave. For example, the dry fly must float on the water, but more than that it must stand upright on the surface film, which isn't quite the same thing. We achieve this by winding a stiff hackle round the head of the fly so that its tiny, individual fibres stand out at right angles from the fly like a frightened porcupine. The dry fly stands on these legs, and the stiffness of the hackle fibre means that the feather should be taken from the neck of a cockerel at least three years old, better four. As such birds are rare, thanks to battery production, the 'necks' are expensive.

The wet fly, by comparison, must sink quickly through the surface film, an act we call a 'good entry'. At the same time it also requires legs to wave attractively below the water. Therefore we need a soft, mobile hackle feather, which at best comes from hens, but also from immature cockerels and the plumage of many game birds like partridge, grouse and woodcock.

An average fly has three parts, tail, body and hackle (legs), to which a wing is often added. For the wet fly, the wing, too, must be low, slim and straight to allow for quick surface penetration as well as the hump-backed shape of

Winged Wet Fly   Hackle Wet Fly

Left:
Streamer: Chief Needabeeh

Right:
Hair Wing: Edson's Dark Tiger

the underwater beetle, nymph, shrimp and what-have-you. Dry-fly wings are often set upright, but since they serve less practical purpose than with the wet fly, modern fly-tyers increasingly omit them. From below, where the fish lies, the wings of the floating fly are largely hidden by the body and hackle, and in fact hackled dry flies catch plenty of fish.

March Brown Nymph

It follows that imitative flies are usually made from dull materials, copying the natural camouflage of the counterpart. We use brown, smoky blues, greys, olives and blacks. Provocative flies are dressed in gay clothing, bright tinsels, fluorescent silks or wools, dyed wings, hackles and tails. Often being larger, many of the latter flies are tied onto extra long hooks when they are generally classed as 'lures' to distinguish them from the normal attractive wet fly. Within this area a confusing medley of names has sprung up, 'flashers', 'attractors', 'deceivers' and so forth, but if you break it down into the two basic types of related feeding behaviour it resolves itself.

Dry flies, wet flies, lures, and then what? The term 'nymph' is used frequently now, both in its precise meaning of the larval equivalent of the group of aquatic insects called 'Ephemera', and also as a loose definition of all under-water forms of life. You hear the water-boatman, which is a beetle, called a nymph, which it is not. The term will stick to a wide range of artificial flies lacking wings, yet being closely imitative of such life-forms as snail, fresh water shrimp, hoglouse, water-boatman, damsel fly larva, buzzer pupa and so forth.

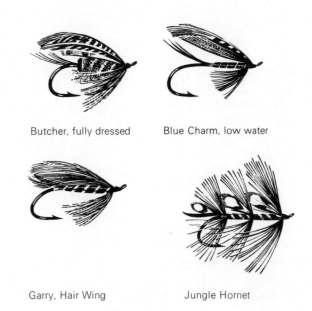

Butcher, fully dressed   Blue Charm, low water

Garry, Hair Wing   Jungle Hornet

So far we've dealt with the broad fly-designs for trout and sea-trout fishing. For salmon, flies divide more simply, but still according to behaviour. Whether or not it could be termed 'feeding behaviour' is debatable, since the stomach of the salmon has little use once his lordship enters fresh water with sex on his mind. We do know that salmon take artificial fly at two levels, quite deep when the water is cold, and just below the surface when the water is warm. The flies are dressed to operate at these levels.

Cold water is typical of 'spring', a time of year when the river is probably in near-flood with barn doors and dead sheep coming down on a snow-broth. The fly is big, usually colourful to show up in the dirty water, and heavily dressed on a big iron, sometimes a double hook. It is cast on a heavy, sinking line.

The flies used in warm water are called 'Low Water' flies, since typical summer conditions are when the water is low and filled with sunshine. The fly is dressed on a thin wire hook. The dressing is quite sparse so that the fly will never sink too much and will move just below the surface. Such flies are fished on a light, floating line, and since these lines needed to be greased to make them float in days gone by, this method is still called 'greased-line fishing', even though modern lines need no such treatment. We meet plenty of such paradoxes in fly-fishing!

Modern fly-tying has given us many new forms of fly, some tied on tubes, others on long trebles, and often animal hair replaces the classic feather wing. The one constant factor is that they conform to the deep-water or greased-line methods of fishing, the former now being termed the 'sunk fly', as if it had been torpedoed.

Both fly-tying and the choice and nomenclature of flies is a wide, specialised subject. There are tens of thousands of different fly patterns. The sensible thing is to delve into the fascinating literature devoted to the subject. It is equally sensible for the beginner to put this frightening complexity out of his mind for now, settling for a basic understanding of how the fish takes the fly, how the fly structure is related to this and then to choose some basic, popular patterns to suit this need, as described later. This is how we start, and no matter how far we stray later it is also how we wind up, for we emerge with a few favourite flies that fill us with hope and confidence, because we caught our first fish on them.

For most fly fishermen, the choice of fly style is dictated by the type of water they fish. This isn't entirely true, because our sport leaves room for eccentricity. Most anglers would fish still water with some type of wet-fly for 90% of the time, but the odd individual may elect to fish all the time with the dry fly only because he finds that style of fishing the most exciting.

Fly Styles

It's usually said that the easiest way to learn fly-fishing is to start with the downstream, wet-fly method because the current will automatically correct faults in casting, straightening out the line. It isn't true, the method being quite different. Unquestionably the novice should stay in the visible world, if he can, and dry-fly fishing is the best school, if only because everything – the rise, the cast, and the fly, the take and the strike – is seen all the time. Although it can reach pinnacles of skill, at its basic level it is far from difficult.

The normal, hackled dry fly is simple in style: two or three whisks are tied in for the tail, the body is usually slim, being made of quill, silk, fur, feather or tinsel, and the legs are copied by winding the feather from the neck of a cockerel round the hook so that the fibres stand out at right-angles to the shank, making a prickly collar. We have always tried to glean these hackles from older birds, which had the stiffest and brightest feathers. Modern floatants are claimed to compensate for the rarity and shortage of such birds, but the weakness of this argument is that the dry fly depends on a high-quality hackle, not merely for buoyancy but also for its posture.

We have seen that fish feed almost by conditioned reflex, and probably the first thing that keys them onto a floating, natural fly are the tiny points of light where their 'feet' pierce the surface film. This effect can be simulated only by a stiff hackle from a cock of three or four years of age. True, we can make the body of a fly float by using a floatant in liquid form, but this is not how the fish sees the natural fly, with certain exceptions.

Daddy long-legs fly tied by the author

Such hackled dry flies copy those naturals which either hatch from the water, returning to it for egg-laying, or those terrestrial insects which blunder onto the surface by accident, such as moths, ants or crane-flies. An exception to the rule of the erect fly would be the female fly, which, after having laid her eggs, dies and becomes the 'spent gnat'. The legs then collapse, the wings stretch out on the water and the body comes right down into the surface film. Yet another exception is the exact moment when the nymph struggles through the surface film, splitting open its jacket to release the adult, winged fly. Fish hit natural flies at both stages and we must copy both the spent gnat and the hatching fly.

Let us start with eggs, on still or running water, from almost every aquatic insect, the Olive Dun, the Cinnamon Sedge, that non-stinging gnat which lake fishermen call the buzzer. These must hatch into some form of larva, which we anglers loosely term 'nymphs', though some are patently not. Fish prey on these larval forms, when they are moving on or near to the bottom, but more especially when they are making their way to surface or bankside in order to hatch into adult flies. The copies of these larvae and nymphs are sometimes exact representations, showing the abdomens, thoraces, gills, emerging legs, wing cases and so on. At other times the copy is more impres-

Top left, Winged Dry-Mayfly
pattern; *bottom left,* a
Tube-fly in the making; *top
right,* finished Sedge-fly;
middle right, a split-wing
version of Dry-fly from
above; *bottom right,*
Dapping-fly (Loch Ordie),
an effective tandem lure

sionistic, as with our standard wet-fly patterns, which have the basic colour and size of the natural, but which when wet depend for their trigger-mechanism on the mobility of the hackle, the humping effect of the wings. From this

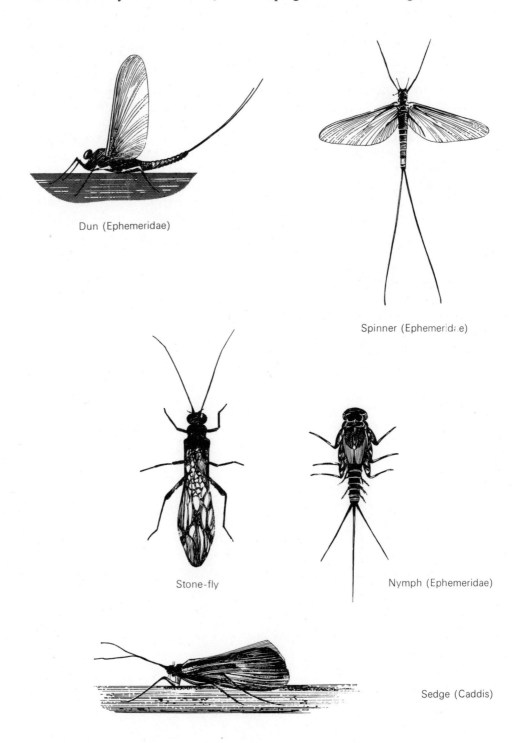

Dun (Ephemeridae)

Spinner (Ephemeridae)

Stone-fly

Nymph (Ephemeridae)

Sedge (Caddis)

arise two distinct styles of fly-fishing on lake and river alike, the traditional wet-fly method and the modern nymph attack.

There are a host of other sub-aquatic creatures on which trout feed, crustacea like the Freshwater Shrimp, beetles like the Water-boatman and so forth. We copy these, too, both purposely with modern imitations and perhaps accidentally with wet flies which are taken by the fish for the natural fauna.

Our true aquatic flies, though, the Olives, the Sedges and the Buzzers, complete their life-cycles by hatching into adult flies. We copy the actual moment of the adult emerging from its larval case with artificials designed to bog down into the surface film, with straggly pieces of fur or feather to create the impression of the legs and wings as they start to emerge from the shuck. A cautionary note here: too many fly fishermen become hooked on the pattern of the artificial being correct in size, colour and shape, while probably the way in which it behaves on or in the water is the most vital factor.

This is the fly in imitative terms, copying the natural fly on the water, whether it be there by purpose or from the land by accident, and copying, too, insects, crustacea, fry and the like under the water. It leaves us only with the group of flies and lures which stimulate a predatory response through flash and movement, the so-called 'attractor' patterns. The attractor fly in all its glory is that used for salmon, which doesn't feed in fresh water in the normal sense of the word but has to be induced into taking a fly, either out of basic predatory instinct or by vague reference to its 'sea-memory' of multi-coloured plankton.

6 Development of the Dry Fly

Having now come to grips with the fly, the method and tools for delivery, we realise that fly-fishing is partly skill and partly ritual. The ritualistic factor enforces the limitations which skill has to overcome and its primary purpose is to protect a primitive creature, the fish, which would otherwise be decimated by easier, 'unsporting' methods such as bait fishing. Ritual results from an evolutionary process and fly-fishing has evolved over two thousand years. We love to remind ourselves of the first record of the art, Aelian's *De Natura Animalium* written in the third century A.D., in which anglers were described thus: 'They love to cover a hook with red wool, upon which they fasten two cock's feathers of a waxy appearance . . . they drop this lure on the water and the fish, attracted by the colour, becomes very excited, goes to meet it, expecting from its beautiful appearance a most delicious meal. As with mouth extended it seizes the lure, it is held fast by the hook and being taken meets with a very sorrowful entertainment.' A perfect description of dry-fly fishing.

The stages of this evolution are marked by the names of famous anglers along the way who have made fundamental changes in method. In 1469 was printed *A Treatyse of Fyshinge with an Angle* by a certain Dame Juliana Berners, which included not only instructions for making rods and horsehair lines, but also listing artificial flies, among them a recognisable popular fly of today, the March Brown, the natural counterpart of which still emerges from rocky border rivers like the Usk and Esk.

After the *Treatyse* there was a spate of angling books, including one by an unlikely Cromwellian Ironside called Franck, who plainly hated his rival Izaak Walton. It is Walton, though, who is revered as the founder of English angling literature, with his *Compleat Angler*, first published in 1653. Walton was an unrepentant bait fisherman, which is probably why his loftier friend, Charles Cotton, contributed the fly-fishing section to the edition of 1657. By Cotton's time distinctive schools of fly-fishing had developed, for while the old *Treatyse* listed but a dozen flies, Cotton named over sixty.

We think these ancient anglers fished downstream, mainly letting the wind blow out the fly on a light line. The rods were very long, up to twenty feet or so. Towards the end of the eighteenth century the reel made its first appearance, from which date rod length could be progressively reduced, and the introduction of silkworm gut was a move towards the modern leader and heavier casting line, no longer at the mercy of the wind.

The shorter rod, the reel and the heavier line with its gut connection to the fly, suddenly released a whole new field of technique, based on the ability to cast the fly upstream. Why upstream? The advantages are in approaching the fish from the invisible area behind their tails, in allowing the flies to wash down to the fish in a natural way and in being able to pull the hook into the mouth of the fish from below. The advocate of the new direction, the voice from the first days of our own century, was the famous Border angler, W. C. Stewart, who laid it down in his book, *The Practical Angler,* that it was an error to fish downstream.

Although Stewart was a wet-fly man, from this revolutionary new theory sprang the whole practice of modern dry-fly and nymph fishing. Stewart fished the Tweed and other Border rivers. The cult of the dry fly was to be born on the crystal rivers of Hampshire, notably the Test, and the High Priest of the cult was to be the great F. M. Halford whose disciples would brook no argument.

It's difficult for us now to recapture the atmosphere of the Halfordian era, at the height of its influence in those golden days leading up to the First World War. What had Halford inherited from the past? Split-cane rods were replacing uncut sections of bamboo, lancewood or greenheart. Heavy, dressed silk lines dictated to the wayward wind. Once again we witness an ironical paradox in that dry-fly fishing was intended to make trout fishing easier and yet became so dominantly ritualistic that it held back the development of new ideas of nymph fishing.

Exact Imitation

Halford concentrated on the natural fly itself, something that had been attempted in only the vaguest way in the past. Stewart's border wet flies were just tumbling bundles of feather in the current. Halford said the dry fly must be an exact imitation of the natural fly as it floats on the water. The Test is no rollicking Border stream. It is majestic, clear and solemn. It's trout are large and selective, having a wide variety of insects with which to preoccupy themselves, a larder being constantly renewed by the alkaline flow. Such leisurely fish could afford to be selective in their feeding, and from such selectivity grew what can only be described as the theology of 'exact imitation'.

Halford's dry flies undoubtedly caught fish. Yet was it necessary to copy minute differences in the sexes of natural flies? And could he expect to imitate faultlessly the delicacy of the natural Mayfly with opaque furs and feathers, tied to steel hooks? It was absurd, but so steeped in absurdity were Halfordians that they banished opposition from the banks of their beloved chalk streams to lesser watery pastures like the Wylie and Nadder in Wiltshire. One such exile was G. E. M. Skues.

The climax of Halford's work, his bible in many eyes, published in 1910, was *Modern Development of the Dry Fly*. The word 'Purism' was applied to those who fished only with the artificial floater, preferably with one of the thirty-three inventions of Halford, tied on the eyed fly-hooks which had been

Dry-fly fishing on the River Colne, Buckinghamshire

made for him by the firm of H. S. Hall. A false Heaven can't last for ever, and in that same year Skues challenged the dry-fly religion with his own work *Minor Tactics of the Chalk Stream*. It's curious to recall that these courteous books were actually descriptions of contrasting fishing methods, and that's all. We cannot now savour the bitterness the dispute aroused.

What was the challenge? Simply put, Skues probably followed the dry-fly habit when he fished the Itchen, much as I do on the Test. You wait, you watch, and when the natural duns hatch on the surface, or the spinners fall, then you fish a copy of this or that fly to the rising trout. In between these short bursts of activity, you wait again. The Itchen is clear, and we assume that Skues noticed trout intercepting the rising nymphs as they came to the surface to hatch. He reasoned that he could imitate these nymphs, fishing them 'wet', usually from below or across to the feeding trout under the surface.

Skues was in every sense a modern angler, fishing dry-fly when indicated, switching to nymph when the surface was quiet. The argument raged, out-living Halford, rumbling on towards the Second World War, after which two disciples of Skues took the nymph technique a stage further. Frank Sawyer, a river keeper on the Upper Avon, simplified the patterns of nymph and widened their range of attack, to grayling, still-water trout and even salmon. His well-known *Nymph and the Trout* revived the nymph art at a time when Skues' ideas were flagging, probably because no new challenge had emerged, and his meticulous nymph patterns were rarely tied. Sawyer was followed by the late Oliver Kite who proved that a trout could be provoked into taking a crude copper-wire covered hook if twitched across its nose, the so-called induced take.

We can say of the great battle that Skues won because the purist school of thought was untenable. Exact imitation isn't possible because our materials for fly-making are too lifeless. Halford worked with quills, furs and feather-fibres dyed in tea, onion juice and picric acid, but he never could capture translucency. Nor could he visualise the way in which a trout sees the fly from beneath the water. His imitations were perfect only in the sense that flies were seen from above in the clear, unbroken light of day.

This isn't the only indictment of 'exact imitation'. Such selectivity implied high intelligence and critical powers of discrimination on the part of the trout. We now realise this isn't the way a trout reacts to the fly. In preoccupied feeding the hatch of a single species of insect sets up the conditioning process and the artificial fly is taken as a reflex. If the fish refuses the fly then for some patent reason, usually in presentation, it fails to trigger off the reflex, and if the cast or the angler is especially clumsy, then the fish is alarmed, either bolting for cover, or hugging the bottom of the stream. It will then be some time before it feels safe to feed again.

No one could deny that Halford started the process of specialisation in fly-fishing, and while his dry flies succeeded by an altogether different mechanism to that which he supposed, they did, and still do catch fish. This being so, fly tyers have given up the battle to give transparency to their dry-flies, realising that when the fish is really locked-on to floating naturals, providing that the basic size, structure, colour and presentation of the artificial is correct, then the artificial will kill in quite a simplified form. The simple form of a modern dry fly, say Kite's Imperial, consists only of a few tail whisks, some coloured herl wound round the shank of the hook for the body, and a stiff hackle feather from a domestic cockerel circling the head so that the fibres stand out at right angles to simulate the legs on which the fly stands on the water.

In all fly-tying we recognise simple formulae for the making of the fly from selected materials. This code was also accepted in the Halford era when exact shades of dye were considered paramount. The code is important for fly-tyers, who remain just a small minority of fly-fishermen. The angler who buys his flies, or has them made specially for himself, must be able to recognise the patterns by their constituent materials. Thus the Imperial would be described thus:

Hook   – size 14 up eye
Tail   – honey-dun cock
Body   – smokey-blue heron herl, redoubled at thorax, ribbed gold wire.
Hackle   – four or five turns of honey dun cock
Tying silk – purple gossamer.

From this simple description the fly-tyer knows how to make the fly and the ordinary angler knows what it looks like when made.

The Modern Approach

We have come a long way from Halford with a fly like the Imperial. Some may dispute that Kite invented it, the fly having been known earlier in Wales. What is true is that in place of a meticulous range of dry flies, each copying its natural counterpart, Kite would catch trout on just two patterns of dry fly on most rivers at any time of the year. His Imperial copied the duns, the Pheasant-Tail Red Spinner dealt with the natural spinners, though this latter fly may be more fairly attributed to Frank Sawyer.

So we come now to those mysterious symbols, duns and spinners. Halfordian doctrines were based on a group of aquatic insects called Ephemeridae, beautiful, gauzy flies with the Mayfly at one end of the size scale, and the tiny, inky Iron Blue at the other. To confuse matters, these flies have two adult stages after the nymphs have come to the surface, cast off their coats to let the adult flies take wing. The first adult stage is naturally heavier, more dull in colour, and the angler thus translates the scientist's 'sub-imago' into the more descriptive 'dun'. After a short time on the wing, the dun sheds its coat too, and the gaily coloured spinner emerges, so named by the rising and falling dance in the air by clouds of males to attract the less numerous females. This is the 'imago' of the text-book.

Hackle-Point Wing Spinner   Hackle Dry Fly   Upright Wing Dry Fly

The mating takes place in the air, the fertile female returns to lay her eggs, the lady then dies, being swept downstream as the 'spent gnat'. Halford, and even Skues, were convinced that it was necessary to dress flies to copy these stages of each variety of the Ephemeridae. Kite discovered that it wasn't. Away from the rich chalk streams of Hampshire, poorer waters produce Stone-Flies, while all rivers have the pent-winged sedges, all of which are taken from the surface by trout, and which can be imitated in the present-day general style, or more closely in the way of Halford and Skues.

Where does the difference lie? In preoccupied feeding the fly has to be correct in size, colour and form. We know today that these factors need to be right in a general sense because the trout is indifferent to minor differences. This is why Kite could group together families of flies which are roughly similar, as are duns in their very drabness and spinners in their gaudiness. He used dull materials to emphasise the factors of the dun, bright silks and hackles to trigger off a reaction to the spinner.

Here I must inject a cautionary note on Kite's simplification. There's some dispute as to whether or not he invented the flies to which he gave his name, though there can be little doubt about the contribution he made to dry-fly fishing by proving that the trout's feeding mechanism was automative. There are yet some natural flies falling outside the scope of his few, simple patterns, notably large ones like the Mayfly, heavier ones like the sedges and altogether different ones like those blown onto rivers from the land, like Hawthorn Flies and Cowdung Flies, two examples of many. The wise angler will steer a course between the two schools of thought, carrying the general patterns for the duns and spinners, plus some extra ammunition for the unexpected or unusual.

My own dry-fly box is made up with hackled patterns to Kite's prescriptions, the Imperials, the Pheasant-Tail Red Spinners, but with the addition of some Sedges, like the Grannom or Skues' Little Red Sedge. I also carry separate patterns for the Mayfly season, plus some 'terrestial insect copies', red and black ants, Hawthorn Flies, Cowdungs, and moths.

I was lucky enough to have been taught fly-fishing by a fanatically purist farmer through whose hop-gardens and apple orchards ran the Wealden River Teise, a meagre stream laced with acid and iron. The trout were small, wild and savage, but dry-fly only was the farmer's rule, which had to be accepted by anyone wanting to fish that part of the river. Looking back, I realise that dry-fly fishing is the best way to learn the whole of our sport, for one very simple reason: you can see what is happening, both to the line and fly, and to the reaction of the fish.

When later you move on to wet-fly fishing, although everything takes place in the invisible world below the surface, because you started off fishing visually you are able to translate what you saw into the areas of touch and feeling. Because he allowed neither bait nor wet fly, the farmer forced me to take it for granted that trout feed on the natural floating fly at times on all rivers and lakes which hold them. What, then, are the consequences of a 'dry-fly only' rule?

Firstly, and above all, you must look for the fish and its rise. This elementary fact alone sends you along the road of learning where to expect the quarry in its natural element, no matter if it be only the mini-warrior of the slow, acid lowland stream or the fast beck tumbling down the Northern Fells. From my own Kentish stream apprenticeship, I first turned my tiny Coachman and Grey Duster dry flies onto the mighty Weirwood reservoir, being a rarity of someone who started his reservoir fly-fishing with the floating fly. Yet it worked, and worked to limit bags. Later, the Test held few terrors to someone whose back-cast was imperilled by bushes and hop-pole wires, whose accuracy in narrow pools had to be able to put a fly onto a postage stamp.

Also, dry-fly fishing at one level is decidedly easy. I well recollect confining myself to the fish in open water when I first began, leaving the heftier opponents secure in their leafy holts. In turn, I soon understood how a trout came to the fly, when to strike and with what force, how to play it out to my feet, for I carried no net in those early times. I soon found out the error of drag, how to cast a wiggly line to avoid it, or when to change the angle of upstream attack to give the fly a clear ride over the fish.

There are other things I didn't so much learn consciously as absorb. The stream was difficult to fish, for not only does it run between high banks, the vegetation of which is over shoulder high in summer, but its character is ever changing, from stickle to slow, deep hole; from long, smooth glides to fast broken water. The trout were by no means plentiful, so that on occasion, in order to get just one shot at a riser, I needed perhaps twenty minutes of preparation, finding the best entry point below, snipping away an offending branch that would have fouled the back-cast, wading quietly upstream to an attack position, though cautiously enough to prevent waves preceding me too far up the pool, or the grating of pebbles, the bolting of fish from lower down.

Relaxation

I discovered, too, the value of relaxation before the cast. Having reached the position after the scramble down the horrifying bank, the stalk forward, then I would wait and watch, noting how the water broke above the lie, where the fly must alight to catch the particular thread of current bringing the naturals into the trout's vision. Then, when all was ready, the still moment of the attack would lick the fly out into the false casts, the eye gauging the distance in the air until it was seen to extend high over the target. Then another cast, high, but if accurate in distance and range the fly would be allowed to fall to the surface, immediately to be picked up by the flow and borne towards the magical spot where it must disappear in the ever widening ripple and bubble of the rise. It taught, and it still teaches because it's positive fishing, none of the hit-and-miss of downstream wet-fly work, with the sudden lunge of the fish, unseen, to be either hooked or free in the twinkling of an eye. Here, I had to set the hook at the fractional pause after that rise.

When Sawyer's book on upstream nymph fishing fell into my eager hands, I took to the method like a duck to water because of my grounding in dry fly fishing. The usual, recommended beginning for the novice is downstream wet-fly because the current mitigates his wayward casting, whereas I had fished dry and nymph upstream, nymph on still water, before I had ever cast a team of wet flies down and across a river.

My personal dry-fly development took me to two other rivers before long, the Whitadder in the Scottish Marches, and the hallowed Test. The former river was one of the stamping grounds of W. C. Stewart, apostle of the upstream spider, yet I saw it as a rather difficult dry-fly water, near to Chernside where I was staying. I must say here that the quality of fly-fishing in Britain has improved in my lifetime to the extent that if many still-water men had to depend on rivers like my own Teise or the Whitadder, they would quickly desert the sport and turn to golf.

Whitadder at summer level was clearer than my native stream, and approach was difficult. Trout bolted from careless casts, rod flash, line shadow, heavy footfall, nylon glitter and the like. This was new to me, as the Teise fish would rise freely provided I didn't alarm them in approach, for the water was always coloured by clay and iron, even at lowest level. To cope with trout in very clear water was a problem new to me, explaining why Stewart started to face 'tother way. And if few modern still-water fishermen don't bother to take on such problems more fool them, because it would teach them more about trout catching than they would ever believe possible.

The Test was entirely different in character, and being the most renowned dry-fly stream in the world needs some comment. At first sight it looks all too easy. The banks are so closely cut as to make bedroom slippers quite comfortable footwear. The stock of big fish in each beat is maintained by periodic reintroduction of fresh trout from the stews. In the two places I fished, at Leckford above Stockbridge, at Bossington below, the river is fairly wide, the current mainly moderate. The water nearly always has a golden tinge so that deeper pools are hard to see into. The surface is strangely knotty, with many whorls, accounting in part for the dominance of dry fly over nymph. It was here, in running water for the first time, where I met the rainbow trout.

Influence of the Rainbow

You can rely on a rising brownie to do two things: to rise steadily during a hatch, and to hold his position. Not so the rainbow. He is capricious, taking a fly here from the surface of a tranquil glide, falling back in a wide circle to reappear on the other side of the river! When first introduced, the rainbow is an idiot fish. It has little natural fear of Man, usually sits in an easy, even ridiculous position, snaps at the first artificial coming over his head, and that's that. The acclimatised rainbow is an altogether different proposition, with his sudden changes of position, moodiness in taking the fly, maybe making a sudden lunge at the umpteenth presentation. Moreover, he's not bothered at all with imitations and has made nonsense of what was written decades ago by Halford and the imitationist school. The rainbow will ignore a stream of Iron Blues, then surge at a piece of floating straw.

I remember well, high in Mayfly time, putting a copy, the Green Champion, to a brownie which never came for it, when suddenly a rainbow charged it from the far side of river, its V-wave clearly shown in its impetuous attack.

The rainbow is inextricably meshed with modern fishery economics, for a river such as the Test has to submit to rod pressure never undergone at the height of the dry-fly age before the First World War. Reading a book of that time, such as Viscount Grey's classic *Fly Fishing,* we have a whiff of a leisurely way of life. He tells us that the chalk streams pall in mid-summer. It's time to be away to the wild places where the mysterious sea-trout roam in the Highlands and Islands. We can visualise the river lying fallow, the banks untrampled by angler and the fish unlined for weeks on end. A fishery like Bossington, probably has at least one rod, perhaps two if a guest is invited, on each of its six beats every summer's day. Only the rainbow put-and-take stocking policy can cope with such pressure. And although the nature of the dry-fly fishing has changed out of all recognition because of the habits of the rainbow, we still read articles written about this river, and others like it, in the old, dry-fly tradition.

This doesn't mean that dry-fly fishing is finished. It does mean that our approach to it has changed, and that today I read Halford and his disciples with modified interest. I was walking back from the bottom of a Test beat in dwindling light when no fish were rising, no fly was on the water, when I caught a glimpse of a rainbow turning deeply in the gloom of a slow, corner pool. I put on a huge moth pattern, the Hoolet, on a size 6 hook, throwing it high into the air to fall with a hefty plop. Up came Mr. Rainbow, engulfed it, and headed for the depths again. I doubt this could be expected of a brown trout, yet it is by no means exceptional of rainbows.

The traditional patterns also intrude, as when I was invited to fish a private stretch of the same river, a part which was but lightly fished. In late September, following a warm summer, trout had gathered at the tail of a gravelly run. I could see clearly some eight large trout in formation, rising as it were in turn to chop off some Pale Watery Duns, those light-coloured flies of the early noon. Working from the largest fish at the bottom of the squadron, I took my limit of five fish from this collection, easing each one downstream under the lightest pressure, for a total weight of over 24 lb. The only fly they wanted, would accept, was a Kite's Pale Watery or his light Imperial, an example of preoccupation and quite easy fishing.

Tackle Considerations

The tackle for dry-fly fishing has already been discussed, the rod having a fastish action. An idiosyncracy of mine, for stream dry fly and nymph, as well as for some boat fly-fishing, is to carry three weights of line, one on the reel-drum, the other two on spare drums. Taking my 'Two Lakes' rod as an example, being normally loaded with an AFTM size 6, I also carry a size 5 and a size 4, the three being double-taper floating lines.

The pleasantest dry-fly fishing is with the lightest possible line, that is the size 4, but it isn't always easy to use, as when the wind is blowing upstream against the current it carries the fly easily, but when pushing downstream against the forward-cast then a heavier line is needed to punch into it. The intermediate size, the DT5, is for the cross-winded or breezy days, for the fault of the lightest line is in its inaccuracy in wayward airs. Casting lighter lines is not too difficult for the man with normal ability. To create rod flexion, the rod has to be driven very hard with strong wrist snap against the blocking action at the termination of the casting power-arcs.

Bearing in mind the strictures against nylon glitter, the ideal fall of the leader takes the last few inches before the fly just under the surface film, so that this part should never be greased. I have been experimenting with black nylon on the assumption that old horsehair leaders may well have been of this colour, and, strangely enough, fish take the fly quite freely even when this leader has passed over their heads. Nylon dyed in silver nitrate solution goes a very dark colour, and is also protected against the oxidising effect of sunlight on the material. Black nylon goes against the recent white-line logic, and while my results are happy I emphasise its experimental nature.

Fly Choice

The aspect of dry-fly fishing which most terrifies the novice is the choice of pattern, and the complexity of entomology. My personal faith in good quality hackle remains because of the pattern of light-points it makes on the surface film, a pattern which, on a stream, the fish must recognise in a split second. The fish makes no choice. Its reaction to that pattern will be governed entirely by conditioned reflexes. If we pass this test, the fish is now moving to the fly, taking its line, and accelerating towards it.

This is the crucial moment of acceptance or refusal, in which colour, size and shape play their part, explaining why fish take the artificial boldly in the diminishing light of dusk. When preoccupied, obviously these factors need to be right, but only in a general sense, for the Olive Dun and the Cinnamon Sedge, for instance, kill fish feeding on a wide range of natural flies of similar size and colour. It's worth knowing some entomology, especially from those books written in angler's terminology, and yet so many fish have fallen from grace because the angler looked at the fly on the water and matched it to the nearest fly in his box.

The type of fishery obviously affects the feeding behaviour of the trout. That acid stream of my youth produced modest hatches, so that the Coachman and Grey Duster saw me successfully through the season. On the Test we have a seasonal progression of flies, from the inky Iron Blue Duns of the raw Spring days, followed by Mayflies when the first dog roses bloom, through to the Olives, Pale Wateries, Sedges and Spinners of Summer and Autumn. Everywhere, though, the local angler, and the keeper in particular, will know what fly will be on the water, and what artificial should be on the end of the leader to match it.

Thus it has always been that an argument has raged between 'imitation' and 'presentation' when fish refuse the fly. It's not as if the trout made an intellectual judgement. At the last minute something simply filters through to the rudimentary brain cells that this isn't food. It might well be some glitter of nylon, some unnatural drag of the fly, and the fish turns away. This isn't alarm. A scared trout bolts for cover, that's all. A fish coming short has rejected the fly as inedible, and there's still the chance to change the angle of attack, to change the fly, to perk up its hackles and have another try.

Now instead of pursuing a dull treatise on the dry-fly art, perhaps you would prefer to accompany me on an expedition to the River Eaulne, in Normandy. This is a tributary of the Arques, that estuary greeting us when the ferryboat arrives at Dieppe. We pass through many picturesque Normandy villages until our host meets us on his own porch. In these same hills and forests he hid during the war, unable to come into his own home because the Germans were hunting him as a Resistance worker whose main task was spotting radar and V1 sites. Today he prefers to stay anonymous, mentioning it but briefly while we sip his ice-cold champagne. Now he takes us to his river, running with a slightly milky colour through lush meadows where browse satin-sided cows.

The Eaulne is a working river. Half way along the stretch it runs slap through a busy farmyard, where a sow sloshes contentedly beyond a rising trout . . . 'The fish are used to it,' explains my friend.

And now the current tumbles down a series of ledges underneath a tangled mixture of brambles and wild roses. There, under the far bank, the Mayfly, wings erect, twitches before disappearing in a happy little boil of water, with a single, golden bubble marking its passing. It's the end of the Mayfly fortnight, when the female spinners are coming back to the water to lay their eggs, which, in their turn will become adult flies two years from now. Then, the task done, these weary flies-for-the-day lay down their wings outright on the water, in dying to become the angler's 'spent drake'.

The artificial fly I now tie on. The body is as white as death, of floss silk, with a fine strand of scarlet floss silk ribbed widely along it, until it reaches the four outstretched wings, asplay, of hackle points. This fly is supported by the lightest of white cock hackles, a mere four turns. If the minutes of love went into my making of it, a second's carelessness could lead to the ruining of it under those treacherous branches. So, watch me make this cast – a narrow loop on the back cast, a late release on the forward throw to turn it over quickly, for a low, fast shoot into the shadow, upstream of the 'plop'.

Down it rides, first under the leaf, then into the shadow, and about now . . . he has it! These Normandy fish are lusty brownies, gold bellied with bright-berried spots on their flanks. Tonight, they will bake well in a sauce of flaked almonds, to be washed down another river in a current of local cider.

The owner invites me to try for the 'bitch', so called because it lies immediately above a stickle of broken-green water, in the very last inch of flow before it tumbles over the lip of rock. The fly must fall within a hairs-breadth of its nose to avoid drag, but, on the back-cast, the line has to be worked through a small gap in the poplars whose leaves already chuckle in a disbelieving wind. You see, the fly lands just right . . . and up goes the rod. He takes it!

Just two nights later and everything has changed. The Mayfly is over, the river quiet as if no trout ever moved eagerly to fly. I know from other seasons that this is the hardest time of all, when fish have just risen from their Mayfly feast, but always there's a chance. In the afternoon, the smaller Olive Duns sailed downstream, unharmed. Some Spinner might tempt them at fading light. And so it is, with the late grass-cutters busy in the meadows, the fish are plopping at the small flies under the bushes in their secret shadows. My Red Spinner proves deadly, even when the shadow is so black I can see no rise nor fly, but must strike to the sound of that succulent plop. Five brownies on the bank, maybe the best going a pound, but didn't they fight with spirit?

This short experience has already revealed how the dry fly, dependent as it must be on observation, is a forcing ground for learning, for without watching, and planning, those fish would never have been taken. I have known skilled reservoir anglers lost on the dry-fly stream, yet the man raised in that style can adapt to any other type of fishing, because his training is a process of tactical response to changing conditions.

Our first dry-fly casts are straight, to easy fish, the period which creates the 'easy method' talk by those who go no further. These easy fish are soon winkled out. The survivors, those in the tricky places and protected by obstacle or drag, become the challenge, raising the standard of the angler to mastering specialised and ambidextrous casts. This is why we start with the dry fly, any many of us intend to end with it.

Later, we will look at the special problems of still-water dry-fly fishing, a sport in its infancy, and exciting for that reason. The delight of dry fly on

streams is that it has such a wide application. It may have developed from the chalk streams, but wild moorland becks, rocky border rivers of Wales and Scotland, sluggish lowland bournes all yield to the method. Not only trout, sea trout and the odd salmon succumb, but grayling, chub and other coarse fish feed on the surface, as witness any Thames weir-run on a summer's evening. As to it being the academy of fly-fishing, I always recall the remark by Captain Marryat, the companion of Halford, that the dry-fly man can adapt readily to every other type of fly-fishing, but the man brought up on salmon fishing would need to go back to school before he could expect success with the dry fly.

7 The Upstream Nymph

We have already seen how upstream nymph fishing developed from the rebellion by Skues against the dry-fly dogma of the early nineteen-hundreds. Earlier we noticed how the development of the heavy fly-line made it possible for the angler to overcome the wind. In short he was given choice of direction in his casting, and it naturally followed that a thinking angler would grasp the advantages of fishing upstream, from behind the trout. This thinking angler was W. C. Stewart, and between him and Skues there lay but a narrow margin, the latter being a natural adaptor of the upstream method to his own conditions and waters.

Stewart fished fast Scottish Border rivers. His flies were scantily dressed spiders, being no more than a thin body of gossamer silk for the body with barely two turns of hackle at the head. Stewart says of these spiders: 'Their great superiority consists in their much greater resemblance to the legs of an insect, and their extreme softness. So soft are they, that when placed in the water the least motion will agitate and impart a singularly lifelike appearance . . . spiders dressed of very soft hackle are more suitable for fishing up than for fishing down, as if drawn against the stream it runs the fibres alongside the hook and all resemblance to an insect is destroyed . . .' It's remarkable to read such an intelligent emphasis on the physical behaviour of the fly in the water, and some decades were to pass before this element was again brought into the structure of the fly, so obsessed had anglers become with exact form and colour. Stewart's spiders placed little value on colour, body and hackle being simple combinations of blacks, browns and reds. They recognised a fact only recently driven home in a scientific treatise on trout behaviour by two scientists, that during their first three years of life, trout recognise their food by its activity.

In the last chapter Skues was presented in his classical rôle of iconoclast to the dry-fly dogma. It is far more realistic to view his ideas as the natural development of Stewart's upstream theory. That Stewart was aware of the Southern dogma is clear from his words, 'Those anglers who think a trout will take no fly unless it is an exact imitation of one of the immense numbers of flies they are feeding on, must suppose that they know to a shade the colour of every fly on the water, and can detect the least deviation from it . . . .' He pours

81

scorn on the notion that trout refuse flies they've never seen before. He was right, because on his fast rivers hungry trout had to seize immediately everything that came their way, quite unlike the portly gourmets of rich Southern chalk streams. Skues was equally right in taking the form and colour of his nymph imitations into closer account.

When we put Skues in contrast to Stewart, then upstream fishing begins to make sense. Undoubtedly they could have fished each other's rivers with success, though the one typified random feeding behaviour, the other preoccupation. Using spider patterns of suitable structure to his tumbling rivers, Stewart was virtually fishing the upstream nymph. Differences there were between his methods and those of Skues, but differences enforced only by the nature of the rivers, not in basic philosophy. The important thing for us today is that we should fish now in almost exactly the same way on the same rivers.

Upstream nymph on a border river

Stewart would soak his gut leader, flies and tip of his line so that they would speedily reach a working depth in the fast flow. He would use a long rod, holding up the line, high in the air so that only the tip would sink with fly and leader. Today we would use a shorter rod with either sink-tip or slow-sinking line. Like the modern upstream expert, Stewart wouldn't need to throw a long line, which would be unmanageable, because he would be stalking the trout from behind. Stewart would cast in such a way as to let his flies fall to the water before the line, for otherwise the current would seize the thicker line belly, dragging the flies downstream at too great a pace. The modern nymph fisherman gives his line a little left-hand pull, pitching the nymph downwards into the water before the line reaches it. This pull is made just as the line straightens over the water on the forward-cast.

Pitching a nymph so that the fly hits the water before the line and leader

The short line, cast upstream, spells out the need for careful stalking, for although the fish are blind to the angler below them, they are sensitive to vibration from any direction. Stewart laid it down 'the nearer we are to our flies, the better we can use them and the greater is our chance of hooking a trout when it rises.' Stewart always used the Royal 'we' when giving personal advice. Let us leave our two pioneers for the moment, to discuss modern upstream technique.

The Approach

Careful stalking is common-sense. The cardinal rules are to avoid clumsy footfalls, grating wader-hobs, falling net-shafts and the like. Avoid allowing your long shadow to precede you up the pool. Sometimes you may be in a diagonal position to the trout, for upstream fishing is not to be interpreted too literally as bank or river-bed contours rarely allow it. Keep as low as you can.

We can still take our two types of river, the chalk stream and the rain-fed Border torrent as typical contrasts. In the latter river, in common with visitors of the last fifty years, we should be 'fishing the water'. This means casting to trout we rarely see, and searching out with our flies the likely places. We seldom see the fish because the water is so fast; we have to approach at a low angle, often by wading, and these rivers are more open to winds which break up the surface into riffles.

How to search the likely places is one of those things that experience teaches and words can only suggest. The rain-fed rivers are often successions of pools and runs. No two pools are alike. Some are deep and slow moving. Others have a fast current tumbling in at the head with a body of almost still-water in the centre, and a fast tail race from the pent-up pressure. Runs usually have a shallow beach of gravel opposite a deep, fast gut of water under-cutting the far bank. Still-depths of pools are often neglected by anglers accustomed to feeling the flies working in the current, but many a fish can be taken by retrieving flies through the pool as if it were a lake.

Casting from the shallow side of a run is easier, the flies being angled upstream to fall within a few inches of the far bank. We would normally start from the bottom of the run, keeping the line straight, by raising the rod tip and taking in line with the left hand. In fierce runs it might be necessary to throw an upstream loop of line immediately after casting to slow down the fly, but with modern, sinking and anti-skate lines, this is rarely necessary. In wintry weather of early season we should fish deeply with larger flies, partly for visibility in water likely to be coloured, but also because fish tend to stay in quieter places when water is cold and heavy. In summer the flies would be fished at shallower depth, even just an inch or two below the surface, and they would be smaller in size.

Surprisingly there's been little sophistication of the spider patterns used on North Country streams since the days of Stewart. The same simple patterns kill as well today as they used to. Personally, I relate the basic colours of my spiders to the seasonal flies. In April I use a brown spider approximating to that early season fly, the March Brown. Remembering our way of coding fly structures, my pattern would be described as:

Hook   – size 12 down eye
Body   – hares' ear, with gold ribbing
Hackle – two turns only of brown partridge shoulder feather

The fur from the hare's ear is truly brown, while many apparently brown furs, such as rabbit, actually have a blue base. The fur is spun round a waxed thread, a process we call dubbing, and the fur-laden silk is then wound round the hook shank to make a smooth furry body.

A summer favourite of mine is the Partridge & Yellow, vaguely to resemble the light-coloured olive flies of that season. The body is merely the yellow tying thread itself, with a gold-wire rib to protect it, wound diagonally along the shank. The legs are as before, two turns of the brown partridge feather. These apart, the usual red or black spiders, local favourites like the Grouse & Orange or Snipe & Purple will kill now as they've always done.

Now let us turn to a Southern chalk stream such as the Test. The basic technique is the same, to fish roughly in an upstream direction, though using the artificial nymph instead of a team of wet spiders. The slower speed of the current makes the nymph effective but rules out the spiders which would be lifeless in most places. Here the trout has more time to inspect food, and has no need to dash to seize passing morsels. Many is the time I've watched a chalk-stream trout let my fly pass by, as if ruminating about it, and then, when past his tail, he's gently turned downstream, returning to take it a yard or two below. The trick here is to resist a heart attack! Apart from this difference in the fly, technique is based on finding a trout, then attacking it visually, much as you would with the dry fly.

Seeing a trout! It sounds so easy. I've a vivid recollection of inviting a guest to replace me on a certain beat of the Test. 'Didn't catch a thing,' he moaned. 'Not a fish in the whole beat.' I took three in the same beat a few days later. This friend was a skilled reservoir angler, unused to hunting down trout in rivers. Brown trout are designed to melt away into their native background, though the foreign importation, the rainbow with its brilliant magenta flank-band, is less able to disappear. Our problem, when looking into water, is that we tend to look through it, focusing on the stream-bed, or its surface.

Visual Attack

The way to search a pool properly requires patience, and absolute stealth in arriving at a vantage point below it. Now look into the water, searching for objects off the bottom, say a sunken branch or trailing weed frond. Focussing on these adjusts the vision to mid-water levels. Next, systematically quarter the pool, carefully moving the height of your head to overcome reflected light from the surface. Polaroid glasses are also useful to reduce surface glare. Chances are that you will discover trout you might otherwise have passed by. It's equally probable that you will be too close to the fish for nymph attack, so line up its position in relation to some bankside mark, say a certain plant or bush, then carefully back off to a casting position.

We have to remember that Skues invented his nymphs in the heyday of the imitative philosophy, so it's natural that his models resemble the native product. They were masterpieces of the fly-tying art, copying in fur and feather the features of the natural nymph, the short protruding tail fibres, the thoraces, gills, wing cases and so forth. They also took from the dry-fly philosophy the attack, not just at a visible fish, but one seen to be actively feeding on nymphs rising up in the water to hatch. The trout which pre-war fishermen would have stalked with the nymph would have been 'bulging'. This means that the fish intercepts the nymph so near the surface that the water is displaced as if the back of the fish were rolling over. We can detect the dry-fly influence in this, the waiting and watching, the casting to a feeding fish with a passable copy, a visible 'take' of the fly and the resulting strike being a reaction to what is seen rather than what is felt.

Yet if you were to join me on the bridge over a chalk stream, where trout can be seen clearly over wide areas, as where the road crosses the Kennet at Hungerford, we would see two other types of nymph-feeding by the fish. The first is typical of the trout lying in mid-water, in the slackish water left by the current bending away from a bridge-pillar. When feeding, this fish will dart out to intercept a swimming nymph, and in so doing the white triangle of the underjaw of the trout is clearly revealed, although no surface disturbance is visible. The nymph fished in the Skues fashion, just below the surface, mightn't induce such a trout to come up to the morsel. The other activity is 'tailing' when a trout is flushing nymphs from weed-beds, rooting them out with his snout well down, and tail sometimes breaking the surface. In the past such fish were thought almost invulnerable to attack by dry-fly or nymph, but no longer.

The difference is simply that today we can use the weighted nymphs, patterns like those used by Sawyer and Kite, which are relatively crude to the eye because a hump of copper wire is essential to their make-up. The place where the weighted nymph has to fall is nicely calculated, so that as it approaches the prey it's falling quickly. As it reaches the fish, the nymph is given a lift upwards in the water, by rod-tip or line pull. These weighted nymphs can be fished upstream to a quarry lying deeply in four or five feet of water. Of all the techniques we've considered here it's probably the most difficult to master. When first I read Sawyer's book I decided to try his methods on the Wealden brook I fished, but the coloured water made actual stalking impossible, and the weighted nymph couldn't be held off the bottom long enough to make 'fishing the water' a practical success. In the end I made nymph imitations with spiderish hackles which would hang in the water for a longer passage downstream. Eventually I was expecting to catch two brace of trout on most of my expeditions. Being a difficult technique, it took some months before the stream taught me to become consistent.

Now why should this be so? In dry-fly fishing we meet a basic simplicity, of casting to a rising fish, then striking when it takes the artificial fly. 'Bulging' trout may be attacked with the nymph in this way, but fish at lower levels are harder to approach because the direction, depth and distance, all have to be computed. Often there will be little surface sign that the nymph has been accepted or refused, which, since the strike must be immediate when fishing in this way, adds considerable perplexity. After a while certain visible signs are appreciated if the line is perfectly controlled as the current catches it, so that it comes back with the stream without slack in it, yet free from unnatural drag through too vigorous a retrieve. The ideal is to have the light source, the sun or brighter area of sky, in front of you, reflected from the leader. Slight checks in its drift, pulls or swerves, all indicate that a trout may have taken the nymph. Trouble is that in most knotty stream-surfaces the leader is affected anyway by movements of water. The nymph in sinking will drag down the nylon, sometimes jerkily as it meets different speeds of flow. The fly may slide off weed-fronds. Only by constant experience can you detect which is a natural check and which is fish.

Types of Nymph

Fortunately some trout can be seen to take the nymph. It may be only a glint below the surface as the trout turns onto it, or the flash of white of the open mouth, and these signs may be struck with confidence. Two golden rules for the beginner are to improve his abilities to see by fishing towards the light source, and to start his nymph-fishing with nymphs designed to hang just below the surface film. While the nymphing trout is less prone to accept a floating artificial fly, the fish taking the natural floaters will often take a nymph offered to him near the surface, for the likelihood is that he is occupied with a hatch of duns. This is, again, a logical step of allowing the visible world to teach us of the invisible, translating sight to touch and even converting it to an instinctive sixth-sense of what is happening in the deeper places.

It's useful to have a quick glance at the natural fly and the artificial nymph. The entomology of such a complex group of insects as the Ephermeridae occupies large volumes. A minority of anglers delve into these mysteries, and it's a fascinating study, but the vast majority are unlikely to recognise the species of a nymph taken from the bed of a river, nor is it necessary to do so for practical angling purposes. Sawyer reduces the complexity of variety to a division based on underwater behaviour. The vast majority of river nymphs are free-swimmers, and the ones with which the angler is mostly concerned. There is a group which crawl on the bottom, particularly in weedy areas. There are flat nymphs which cling to the undersides of rocks and stones, and finally those which burrow into silty beds, giving fish little chance to hunt them down.

The large Mayfly nymph is of the tunnelling variety, and when ready to hatch it comes directly from its hole to the surface, which explains why, when trout take this nymph, it gives us the classical bulging rise near to the top. Few anglers like fishing with the Mayfly nymph, for in their short hatching season at the end of May the dry-fly man has a fortnight of superb fishing with duns and spinners. On the Test at Bossington, where I had a rod for several years, during a hatch of duns the trout had the frustrating habit of hitting the nymph just before emergence.

On this fishery the 'dry-fly only' rule applied. At first it was hard to understand what was happening because my companion and I could see the duns sailing along unmolested at the same time as the water was being broken here and there in savage whorls indicative of a surface rise. The artificial fly was refused stubbornly. By watching a fish closely I soon spotted what was happening, and, and, to cut the story short, I caught him by clipping closely the hackles of the dry fly and throwing it hard at the trout's nose as soon as he came up to chop off another emerging nymph. This proves the occasional value of a 'hatching nymph' pattern of fly, copying the exact position of the nymph in the surface film itself, at the precise moment when the shuck will split open and the adult dun appear. All that's necessary is to take the normal dry-fly equivalent and clip short the hackles to form a stiff collar of bristle to hold the fly in that surface-film position.

A happy discovery is that nymphs partially resemble their respective adult duns. If you take the small, inky Iron Blue, one of our commonest Ephemeropterans, its nymph is also small and of a very dark, slaty colour. In the north, spiders like the Snipe & Purple or the Waterhen Bloa with its mole's fur body, are taken by trout for Iron Blue nymphs. Skues would have satisfied himself with a careful copy of the nymph, but today we rarely discover an acceptable true copy. In fact both Kite and Sawyer have reduced nymphal imitations to relatively crude examples of fly-tying to serve their needs for quick sinking and inducing the 'take'. If you wanted a precise copy of the Iron Blue nymph, you could possibly get by if you clipped away the hackles of the dry fly, then soaked the body to make it sink. Or you could dub mole's fur onto a size 14 hook, thickening it up for the thorax with a dark feather-strip over the back of this small hump to copy the wing-cases. Do the same thing with fur from a hare's ear and you have a March Brown nymph, though the hook would be larger. Using olive materials, you have an Olive nymph, while light grey fur or herl would yield up the Pale Watery nymph. All of these may have a wire rib, or even a turn or two of fuse wire under the thorax to assist clean penetration through the surface.

Personally, I sophisticate the famous Pheasant Tail nymph, named after the fibres from the cock pheasant's tail. Choosing a reddish centre-tail feather, I tie in three for the tail whisks, winding the rest up the shank to form the abdomen of the nymph, over which is ribbed a fine copper wire. A bunch of the fibres is wound on to make a knob just below the hook eye, for the thorax, and another six fibres brought over the top of the thorax to simulate the wing-cases. Of course it has been proved that such sophistication is unnecessary for the 'induced take' way of provoking a trout, but I'm emotionally suited to waiting for fish to move to surface fly or nymph, and even though I normally have a rod on one of the chalk streams my trips are sporadic enough for me to indulge myself in dry fly, or imitative nymph fishing just below the surface.

We have seen the unity between the upstream wet flies of northern rivers, and the more careful nymph attack in the south, and noted the greater versatility of the latter, if only because teams of wet flies cast in any direction would be forbidden on chalk streams. The upstream nymph, though, is effective outside of the country which gave it birth. I have applied it to the rivers of Scotland, Wales, Eire and France.

Technique

When instructing in fly-fishing I've been struck by the border-line between facts, as in casting, for example, and the river beyond where the beginner must eventually learn how to apply what he has been taught. A strange thing that happens to me is that I can stay away from dry-fly work, still-water, sea-trout and salmon fishing with no great harm, but this isn't so with nymph fishing. Those seasons when I was able to go regularly to the river with only a small box of nymphs in my bag also witnessed the catches steadily mounting, and yet it only needed a few weeks lay-off to reduce me to a fishless wreck until the old familiar rhythms returned. This is no superstition, for the qualities that fall away are tangible.

In comparison to dry-fly fishing, the exact place to drop the nymph is tricky. Suppose you're casting to a fish above you on the far bank: if it were a dry-fly you would false cast until you'd estimated that the fly would fall onto the stream a foot or so above the rise. The nymph, though, would cut through the surface to hang on the leader, perhaps at a depth predetermined by the application of mucilin. For example, if you want the nymph to sink to about a foot, you grease the nylon to that point above the fly and occasionally clean the last twelve inches with detergent solution. It also means that you must allow an extra foot or so beyond the fish as well as above, so that in sinking the nymph will line up with the quarry.

Having made the cast and pitched the nymph through the surface, the left hand immediately takes up the slack line, bunching it with the fingers of the left hand. This line control is also to be finely calculated. With the dry fly, some slackness can be whipped up on the strike and may even help to prevent drag on the fly by cushioning the speed of the current. In nymph fishing the strike has to be an immediate response to the take of the fish, and, drag being less of a problem, the line needs to be kept as straight as

Retrieving line by figure-of-eight bunching to keep in touch with the fly

possible. Alas, it's so easy to overdo this and pull the nymph through the water in an unnatural way. These finer adjustments are the points to be finely honed by continual practice, and knowing this I accept the argument that nymph fishing is ethical on rivers which, in the past, were reserved for dry fly.

Presumably, numerous anglers give up nymph fishing because they fail to grasp the need for a fairly long initiation period. I persisted because I was excited by Frank Sawyer's book. It was an unexplored world. I was able to relate some past failures with the dry fly on bulging trout. Even so, I recollect that two or three trips to the stream I was fishing in Kent produced no fish! Then it began to happen. A fish or two would fall victim, then next time three, until in high summer, when dry fly was beyond hope, I could expect to fill the bag. Of course I had to adopt the patterns invented for clear-water streams in Hampshire to the small, stained water of Sassoon's country, as I was pretty sure that it was exactly the same brook he described in his famous memoirs of fox-hunting just before the outbreak of the First World War.

Skues, Sawyer and Kite described the stalking of trout in clear water, which not only could be seen but were sometimes even seen to take the nymph. I may well have been the first Sawyer disciple to apply the upstream nymph to trout that were rarely seen, and even when taking surface food left only their tell-tale ripples on the water.

The trout which pleased me most during this apprenticeship was rising in the smooth glide at the tail of a pool just before the water broke up into a roiling stickle. As soon as the line hit this fierce little run the fly must drag. The cast had to pitch the nymph almost into the trout's mouth for it would ride cleanly for but a fraction of a second. I made the cast precisely with a small Hare's Ear nymph, the leader pulled down according to classical description, and a furious half-pounder was mine. What contented me in retrospect is that I had thought the problem out in an entirely new perspective, in terms of depth, distance and direction, whereas before that time I had fished *with* what I could see *to* what I could see.

The rain-fed rivers have another contrast to the chalk streams. On the latter you feel a cycle of activity building up to a hatch of fly, and you can match your mood to it. They provide benches along the banks where you can relax until the momentum begins. The nymphs key themselves up for hatching, emerging or swimming to weed fronds up which they climb towards the surface. This is the underwater world of the trout and the excitement communicates itself to the fish. The angler, looking down the river, sees firstly the odd dun drifting here and there before the main-stream of them starts to come down. The occasional plopping rise will now appear. This process will progressively build up to the steady hatch, with trout either taking fly off the surface or below it.

We cannot comprehend the causes of the activity, probably being subtle changes in atmospheric pressure, intensity of light or oxygen content of the water. We know that in summer it may start in the forenoon and that morning activity is rare. In early and late season the rise may well begin during the morning, especially of those flies which relish the cold airs, the Iron Blues, March Browns and Early Olives.

This isn't true of the poorer rivers where hatches are capricious. My success or failure often depended on whether or not another angler had disturbed the water before I started to fish. Sawyer had written that unless you could see either fish or his take you had little chance of catching a trout on upstream nymph. I had to pitch my nymph in places where I hoped trout might be. I shall never forget one particular cast which brought the fly through very fast water by an undercut bank where, at a certain point, I struck a fish only because I thought he ought to be there. So fast was the flow that the leader itself couldn't be seen. The line was kept straight enough to make contact as the fish shot out from his hidden lie to seize my nymph. A second longer and he would have rejected it, for lean, wild trout in such places are conditioned to keeping food and rejecting foreign objects in the twinkling of an eye.

I've now designed a rod specifically for nymph fishing, the 9′ 3″ 'Professional'. As the normal dry-fly rods are not fast enough in their tip-action, I load my new rod with a floating line, one or two sizes lighter than normal, either DT 5 F or DT 4 F. The double-taper fly line is essential for achieving the true pitch of the nymph whereby it curves downwards to the water before the line. The weight concentrated in the head of a forward-taper line destroys this effect. Even with line sizes above 6 it's impossible to present either nymph or upstream spider efficiently.

Detecting the 'take'

The leader plays an important part in nymph practice, for in addition to its usual service of delivering the fly, it's often the only guide to detecting the 'take'. Nylon normally has a surface which reflects light, but in some conditions of light this transparent material becomes invisible, for camouflage is part of the line-maker's appeal. I was reading some old fishing magazines in which there was a discussion on the use of black nylon for leaders or leader-points. I was fortunate in finding some black nylon in Germany, but for anyone wishing to follow my own experiments, nylon takes up a dye readily, while silver nitrate, in solution, also darkens it. My conclusions are that black nylon doesn't worry fish any more than normal leader material, and that in conditions of light which make it hard to see transparent leaders, dark ones may often be a more efficient indication that the nymph has been accepted.

Rules vary from fishery to fishery, and restrictions of method are usual on chalk streams. On rain-fed rivers, as distinct from chalk streams which are mainly spring-fed, rules are more liberal, and you may be allowed to fish a combination of nymph and dry fly. A dry fly on a short dropper serves two purposes. It determines the depth at which the nymph is fished, for if the dry fly is a foot from the leader-point, then the nymph can work down to this depth. It may sound sacrilegious, but the dry fly also serves as a bite indicator or float. In fact it acts as a guide to the position of the nymph and leader, especially in fast or broken water, for a trout taking a nymph at a foot or less below the surface should leave a marked disturbance of the water.

The careful use of mucilin on the leader is essential in nymph fishing, to grease the nylon which is intended to float. This grease has a way of trans-

The author waits and
watches for rising fish on the
River Teise, Kent

ferring itself in casting to the whole of the leader, so that it's wise to carry a
small bottle of detergent or soap solution to clean off the last few inches of
the leader, at least to the depth you choose for the nymph to fish. This sounds
finicky, but it's better than being stuck with a nymph which simply refuses to
sink quickly enough. The amount of equipment carried by the nymph fisherman is compact, for the range of fly patterns is limited, due to the policy of
creating an impression of activity with the fly, rather than making a careful
deception as with the floater. True, we may enjoy taking the artificial to a close
resemblance of its natural counterpart, but the success of Frank Sawyer with
his simple fly-dressings proves it to be unnecessary at a strictly practical level.

8 The Still-water Scene

The development of specialised techniques for still-water fly-fishing has been a comparatively recent phenomenon. It has lagged behind the provision of facilities for trout fishing by public authorities in vast reservoirs. The reasons for this delay are hard to fathom, except what when the fly fishing community was smaller river fishing was generally more popular. Most lake fishermen were content to use standard wet-fly patterns in larger sizes, a habit spreading from Scotland which caused these old favourites to be classified as 'loch flies', even if they were to be used in Somerset.

There were always brown trout in many lakes in England, in Scottish lochs, Welsh llyns and Irish loughs before someone hit on the idea of stocking an artificial lake. The first of these to make a reputation was Blagdon, a water-supply reservoir for Bristol set in spectacular scenery in the Mendip hills. It opened for trout fishing before the First World war and inside the rustic lodge are glass-cased monsters of such vintage years as 1910. In some of these cases the successful flies are exhibited, many of them huge salmon lures such as might grace the Spey in spate.

Blagdon set two fashions: the first was stocking still-water fisheries with the rainbow trout, and the second was the provision for trout fisheries in succeeding new reservoirs.

Rainbow trout aren't native to Britain. They were introduced from North America. Even though the first rainbows came to Britain over fifty years ago, surprisingly little information is available on their acclimatisation, and even this little amount is at a practical fish-management level, not scientific in nature. The rainbow is popular with anglers and fishery managers alike because it is fast growing, in spite of a short life span in comparison with our native brown trout. For the same reason it is cheaper to buy from our commercial fish farms, the oldest of which dates back 85 years when artificial restocking of fisheries began in Britain. The rainbow trout takes the fly more eagerly than his brown cousin and often fights with greater verve, usually making spectacular leaps into the air. It's reasonably hardy, but except in rare places cannot reproduce itself naturally in Britain.

It must be admitted that the rainbow is far less discriminating in its taste than the brown trout. When fishing lures and flashy wet-flies, rainbows noticeably figure higher in the catches, and the contrary is often true when using strictly imitative flies and methods. The trend has been for the stocking proportion of rainbow trout for still-water to grow larger in proportion to brown trout, and even on chalk streams the same trend is happening. Lastly, even though the rainbow, in common with all trout, takes the general coloration of its background, because it isn't indigenous to our fisheries it's much easier to find. Sideways on, the bright magenta flank-band can scarcely be hidden, while caudal and dorsal fins are heavily freckled with dark-brown spots. As it grows older the fish reddens up like a salmon that has long rested in fresh water.

Another problem of 'put-and-take' stocking policy, as the continual replacement of caught trout is called, is that many lakes have no population of purely wild trout. One of the heated debates in angling today is the extent to which farm-bred rainbows are easy game because they have never developed the native wildness of creatures born in a tooth-and-claw environment. Indeed, until planted out into the lake, Man is recognised as the friend who brings the food. The food is in the form of a small brownish pellet, and for some time after being released in a lake, flies resembling pellets easily catch rainbows. It has been shown that once trout have been reared in stews on these food pellets they will come to them eagerly again, even months afterwards, if thrown to them in their supposedly newly-acquired wild state.

The hard truth is that this is how fishing must be, so intense is the demand for it. Nor should we be too despondent because even these artificially reared rainbows learn some degree of wariness, given time. The effect of constant fishing, with trout being pricked occasionally, lost from the hook, or scared by rod-flash, clumsy wading and casting, is to make a hard core of wary survivors from each stocking. An older angler may sigh at the prospect of the fishery manager being pleased to see his customers catch fresh stockfish too easily, but the modern world requires the one to satisfy the other. We can only hope that still-water fisheries will always put in a proportion of brown trout, and never rely entirely on the 'put-and-take' rainbow policy. I should hate to see the red and grey squirrel situation being applied to our fisheries on trout terms, and it would be a sad thing indeed if our children grew up never to encounter our native brown trout.

Modern Tactics

After the Second World War reservoir trout fishing expanded, the provision of impounded water for domestic and industrial consumption matching a desire to landscape reservoirs into the rural scene and also to provide increased leisure activities for a tension-ridden urban community. The pace of life accelerated, standards of living gave nearly every family a car and the desire grew in the hearts of ordinary people to share those pleasurable activities which, though envied, their fathers never had the opportunity to enjoy.

Some of these reservoirs were in groups to supply industrial areas, such as those clustered around Northampton, at Eye Brook, Ravensthorpe, Pitsford and Grafham, the mightiest of them all, a veritable inland sea. These were opened to the angling public on a day or season-ticket basis, while smaller ones, such as Hanningfield in Essex or Bough Beech in Kent, were available on season permit only.

Although occasional books cropped up, dealing with loch fishing, it was not until the Northampton reservoirs made their impact that a distinctive still-water fly-fishing school emerged, the philosophy of which was first compiled in T. C. Ivens' book *Still Water Fly-Fishing*. This was based on the long, butt-actioned 10-ft. rod, which has been largely outdated by new thinking on distance casting from the shores of extensive lakes. The book was revolutionary in its time for various reasons, not least of which was the emphasis on the 'ordinary man's trout'. Looking back, one has the impression of men back from the forces, building up new lives on a tight budget yet determined to get the best out of the trouting opportunities offered by the new lakes. It was implied that boat fishing was too expensive. It was discovered that good bags could be made from the bank if only the angler were able to throw a long line.

It was at this point in time that practical angling began to develop a separate distance cult, distinct from tournament casting, and virtually having no dialogue with competitive casting experts, a situation which continues to exist in Britain. This explains why these early distance techniques were inefficient, dependent as they were on power of tackle and muscle.

The new fly patterns, by contrast, were of lasting value and a complete departure from those used previously, suited to the idea of drifting a boat down a long wind-lane while a team of wet flies was worked through the top few inches of water. The new family of flies were imitative in only the vaguest sense, but they were designed to operate at chosen depths, from surface, mid-water to near to the bottom. They were streamlined in shape to serve the need for distance casting. They were called 'reservoir nymphs', using the term in its widest meaning because the shape of the new flies was roughly similar to that of the stream nymph, similarly shaped for swift penetration of the water.

Invaluable though this development was, giving an entirely new philosophy to still-water fly-fishing, it didn't go far enough. It added a new dimension, but made no concession to an angler who wished to explore beyond the mechanistic limits of casting and retrieving the fly. It decried the possibility of the dry-fly, restricted lure fishing to a single pattern, the Jersey Herd, while the whole field of imitative fly-fishing was neglected. It has been estimated that in some lakes a single family of non-stinging gnats, known scientifically as Chironomidae and colloquially as buzzers, accounts for up to 70% of trout diet. In reading accounts of the development of fly-fishing in the early years of the Midland reservoirs we are forced to concede that, at that time, there was no imitative attempt to profit from the appearance of buzzers.

This isn't a criticism of those who first started still-water specialisation. We have seen previously that river fly-fishing developed slowly over a much longer period. Reservoir fly-fishing in particular, and at a popular level, is a comparatively new sport. After the interest was aroused, well-known fly-tyers, such as Commander C. F. Walker, and entomologists like John Goddard made close studies of the insect life of lakes and invented deceptive imitations of this life at its various stages, in or on the water.

The serious angler must concisely understand the basic framework of trout food in still-water. Using the term 'insect' loosely to define the variety of small creatures on which trout feed, be they crustacea, insect, true bugs or beetles, this life has a cycle much as it does in rivers. Lakes in different geological conditions hold different types and ranges of insect life; chalk, for example, helps form the hard-shelled fauna like snail and water-boatman.

Trout Behaviour in Lakes

Life is dormant in lakes during the winter until the increased hours of sunlight warm the shallow areas, causing a flare up of the microscopic plant life which forms the lowest link of the food-chain. Colonies of small animals, the zooplankton, then increase, followed by their predators, the insect world, which awaken and multiply to attract the attention of the fish. The natural food of trout is rich in protein, but the supply of protein in a lake is dependent on the microscopic plants (phytoplankton) to use the sun's energy fruitfully when its strength reaches a certain level. This turns on the ability of the sun's rays to penetrate clear water, and it explains why a very deep water with no balancing shallows makes a poorish trout fishery.

During the cold times of the year trout are inactive Their slow growth in low temperatures is clearly shown on one of their scales, the reading of which under low magnification determines the age of the fish. The scale is marked in bands, wide bands being summer growth, narrow bands being winter growth. Fastest growth lies within the temperature range of 55 to 65° F. When water temperature falls to 35°F. the fish will rarely feed, but as it rises progressively the tempo of feeding and digestion also quickens. At the top end of the scale, appetite begins to fall away over 65°F., and deaths of the trout are possible from 70°F. upwards, depending on the amount of oxygen in the water. I carry a thermometer in my fishing bag to give me an idea of the expected levels and times of trout activity.

The exception to the rule is the predatory instinct of the rainbow trout, which will still chase and seize a lure even though water temperature is very low, and it's this habit of what might be termed a non-feeding response to colour and flash that makes the rainbow so vulnerable to the bright lure so early in the season. This is why lure fishing is quite distinctive from other fly-fishing methods, and is intended to provoke the random-feeding response, even when fish wouldn't normally expect or need to find food.

In 1970, when able to participate in the making of the new lake trout-fishery, at Sundridge, in Kent, I obtained a different slant on the acclimatisation of the rainbow trout into still-water. One fact stands out – these fish will eagerly chase a brightly coloured lure within a few minutes of being introduced into bitterly cold weather. They will be as easily caught a few days later, having by then been converted to that horrid, blackened appearance of early-season rainbows recently introduced into cold water. If killed and opened, the fish rarely contain any normal food, and I have known trout go for three weeks after April stockings without feeding normally, yet still chase after lures.

These lures aren't normal flies, nor even are they imitations of small fish. They are brightly coloured, having bodies of silver or gold tinsel, hackles of

A nice rainbow trout from Sundridge, Kent, but note the tail is eroded, typical of concentrated trout-rearing in stew ponds

Early-season rainbow, blackened and in poor condition. Caught in April, they might well have recovered by May if they had been returned to the water

dyed feather and wings of coloured fur or feather. Their success in early season often converts the angler to using the lure, and nothing but the lure, right through the summer months when greater pleasure would be gained from imitative tactics. Over newly flooded land, when a new reservoir is made and has little chance to develop its own aquatic fauna, rainbows grow quickly on worms trapped by the floods. They are also frenzied takers of the lure. When Grafham was opened I used to watch a boat fisherman whose method was to hurl out a team of multi-coloured tandem lures on a floating line. These he would strip in as fast as he possibly could, while the rainbows would chase them through the water like Miura bulls trying to nail Manolete! As this was typical the opening of Grafham changed the perspective of still-water fly-fishing, bringing the use of heavy tackle and the stripped lure into prominence.

We are still living with this changed perspective today, and while I'm not opposed to the lure on lakes I dislike the indiscriminate and continuous use of the lure in contrast to intelligent tactics. I use the lure myself when it appears to be indicated, but much prefer to fish with some finesse, deceiving rather than provoking the fish. As for the heavy equipment, that is the Avon or even Carp rod-blank, converted for fly use with very heavy lines or shooting heads, since these can horse-in 4-lb. trout, then one of the greatest pleasures of fly-fishing is lost, that of fighting a fish against responsive tackle. Or are we all becoming fishmongers?

Let me defend my use of the lure on occasion. Twice have I fished different reservoirs on autumn days cursed by strong winds. At one the anchor wouldn't even hold the boat on the lee shore. Days previously the fattened rainbows had been harrying fry along this particular bank, but I would expect both the small fish and these trout to be scattered from the weed beds there by the turbulent water, which had also coloured up from bank erosion. It struck me that the fish would still have the taste for fry, but that something a little brighter than a normal minnow-fly would show up in the cloudy water. I borrowed a whitish lure from a local expert.

The local expert took an early brownie along one marginal shallow, and a second rainbow in the afternoon while I was trying to steady the boat into the teeth of a gale for him to make a reasonable cast. Later the wind fell away and we found some slightly calmer water in a lee shore, calm enough at least for the anchor to hold us. Beyond was a shallow bay where earlier trout had been caught in herding the fry towards a stream entrance. They should have scattered from there into this wider area of deeper water. I was using my 'Powercast' rod with the 'Fast Taper' sinking line, easier to manage in high winds than a shooting head and not far less in performance. I rolled it down-wind about twenty-five yards, letting it work deeply. I twitched it back very slowly, being a strong believer in the slow-retrieve, even with lures. Until then I'd no fish to show for the blisters on my palms, but here I collected a brace – good enough for such terrifying squalls.

A fortnight later, at the second reservoir, a force five wind was ploughing white furrows along the dam-wall. Suddenly the yellow stream of a local river began to flow into the corner of the dam, for this was one of those reservoirs where levels are maintained by pumping from the nearby river. I thought the

The busy banks of the Chew
Valley reservoir, Somerset, do
not prevent the occasional
trout catch

A rainbow lunges from the
net at Grafham reservoir,
St. Neots, Bedfordshire

surge of water would blow up from the bottom a whole host of bloodworms, as we call the larva of the buzzer. These bloodworms should attract small fish, which, in their turn would be preyed on by trout. The water was turbid from the inflow, so a bright lure had to be retrieved slowly on the bottom. The third cast produced the savage wrench of a hefty rainbow, soon bouncing on the boards of the boat. When opened at home it was full of bloodworms . . . and small fish!

Tactical choice based on trout's feeding behaviour: a fish is seen feeding on bottom fauna while, above, another trout intercepts nymphs or beetles on their way to the surface. At the surface one trout is taking nymphs as they hatch and another leaps into the air onto adult floating flies

You will understand from what has been written that still-water fly-fishing can be enjoyed at a primitive level. The lure fisherman can apply his method right through the season, casting to his limit, retrieving a favourite pattern of lure and letting the catches average out. The boat angler can fish his drift, letting the boat run before the wind while he plies a team of familiar wet flies in front of the boat. He, too, will have his red-letter days when trout are moving just below the surface, to take his tail fly as a rising nymph or pupa, or to seize the buzzy bob-fly as he dibbles it on the surface like a hatching fly. These routines don't solve all of the problems of still water fishing. The difference is that these two anglers, the lure stripper and the boat angler, have decided in advance how they will fish without taking into account the prevailing conditions.

Tactical Choice

The tactical approach to still-water has a simple basis. It means that you will *never* decide in advance how you will fish the water. You decide when you see or sense what is happening. The two obvious physical factors are the wind and light.

Most of our reservoirs have very deep areas in front of the dam wall. Deep water stratifies into an upper layer of warm water, a lower layer of cold water with a layer of rapidly changing temperature between the two. known as the thermocline. This thermal stratification happens in the summer according to the penetration of sunlight. Its effect on fish is little understood. It was commonly thought that trout couldn't survive below the thermocline where the amount of dissolved oxygen was too small, but echo-soundings have revealed shoals of fish well below thermoclines in some lakes.

A constant wind tilts the layers of water towards the shore on the windward side, so that warm water piles up there, while along the lee shore cold water from below the thermocline may be exposed to the surface. At a point from the lee shore the two layers merge, and on summer evenings I try to guess the location of exposed thermocline because the trout learn to love it. I imagine this is because it's refreshing to them after being confined to warm, bright upper layers. Whatever the reason, there's a mingling of the warm water with the cooler, with sufficient dissolved oxygen, and in these areas of contrasting conditions trout and their prey are active. I have yet to read a research study on the effects on trout of these thermal layers in summer and the movement of them by the wind, but from a practical fishing point of view the lee shore in a gentle ripple is often the most productive part of a deep lake or reservoir in periods of summer heat.

Watching the water is obviously a precondition of tactical choice. I mention here the recollection of the many times I've witnessed an angler fishing blindly with sunk line and lure while close by, unnoticed, fish were moving near to the surface. I carry a pair of German binoculars with a magnification of eight. They are miniaturised, and flat enough to fit comfortably into the pocket of my fishing coat. Though expensive, they are one of the most important items of my equipment, especially on a wide expanse of water. They are used in two ways, to pick up areas of activity at long range, as for example an area of

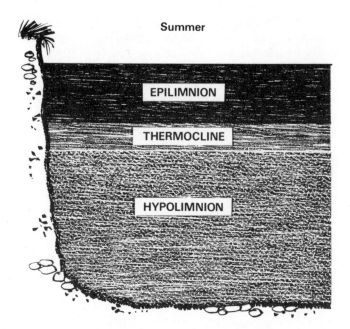

Summer

EPILIMNION

THERMOCLINE

HYPOLIMNION

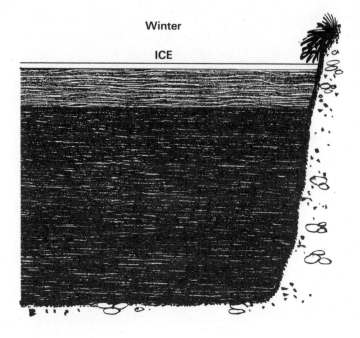

Winter

ICE

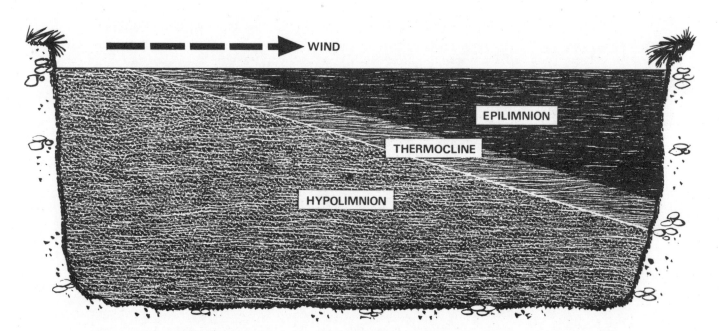

WIND

EPILIMNION

THERMOCLINE

HYPOLIMNION

martens swooping on hatching flies, and at closer range to identify possible rises.

When fishing with novices, the handicap they reveal is the inability to see rising fish. On a flat calm the signs are clear enough, but in a ripple or wind lane the most we may see is slight push of the water against the wind. When

Above, thermal stratification of a lake in summer compared with uniform temperature below ice in winter; *below,* thermal layers tilted by a wind in summer

a trout swallows a nymph under the surface the tell-tale sign is not the familiar, ever widening ring, but merely a displacement of the surface water.

Even when the rise is sharply defined, one thing the binoculars reveal is the direction in which the trout is moving. Many anglers blandly assume that trout feed into the wind. Closer observations prove this to be no invariable rule. Frequently trout move across the wind to take a fly, even pursuing skittering insects downwind. If fish-watching were a hobby like ornithology we should know far more of their behaviour. It's extremely difficult to know in which direction a fish is moving when watching a surface rise. It is as if the elipse of the disturbed water had a sharpish end, showing the direction of the trout, whereas the side of this elipse which is flattened is the fin-mark of its passing. This makes sense on reflection, because the rise is a cleavage of the surface by nose and dorsal fin.

Nor is it sufficient to detect the rise without making an assumption as to its type and cause. Again, there's no substitution for observation, aided by the glasses. In chasing fry, trout often break surface in fury of pursuit, which can

Anticipating the direction of a trout from its rise

easily be mistaken for a slash at surface fly unless the smaller arrows of fleeing tiddlers are spotted at the same time. The rise to floating flies is either of a bubbly 'plonk' to a sedge, a gentle sip to a small trapped insect or a zig-zag furrowing of the water after a skittering fly. The nymphing trout displays either a leisurely wiggle through the surface film or another sipping rise to a pupae hanging in that same film, prior to hatching.

This question of seeing the fish, with the interpretation of what you see, is most important in still-water work because, when fishing with the floating line on, or close to the surface, the interception of the fish with the fly is the make or mar factor. Without intelligent observation, the fish could be moving anywhere through 360 degrees. The reflex action is to cast the fly directly into the broken surface, but this is where the fish has just been, rarely where he's going unless the hatch is concentrated in a small area. A cruising rainbow may have travelled several yards while your fly is on its way to that rise mark. On occasions when fish accept a fly fished into the 'boil' it may well be that it's the tail-ender of a small cruising pack, not the chap who made the original break.

Very boring it may seem to waste good fishing time in watching trout, until you grasp one elementary lesson – a rising trout is also a moving target! Only then will you learn to compute distances and directions from rise to rise, to assess the beats of certain trout or the cruising patterns of the passing rainbow shoals. If the subject is emphasised here, it's because river trout have defined lies, dictated by food-flow and current. No similar conditions influence still-water trout.

Unseen Areas

The problems of dealing with the surface rise on lakes are interesting enough. It may be that for the most part of the day there's no surface activity whatsoever, and the fish, if feeding, will be doing so on, or close to the bottom. This is the most trying time of all, when the water is inscrutable, unmoving. It happens in very bright conditions, or when the upper layers are chilled by a cold wind. We must assume in any case that only a small proportion of fish will be feeding high in the water, the larger number on or near to the bottom, and the temptation is to conjure up a mental picture of trout confined to layers, which is often nonsense, as when fish flush larvae or nymphs from deep weed-beds, then chase them to the surface. One temptation, when nothing is seen, is to tie on a lure and flog away with the deep-sinking line.

A better ploy is to fish the nymph deeply, using the word 'nymph' in its wider angling sense to mean almost any fauna-imitation appropriate to the water. Knowledge of this fauna may be difficult to come by. For the occasional visitor, the simplest solution is to ask either the bailiff or regular anglers the types of trout-food active at that time and place, something they will know from cleaning or spooning out their catches over periods of time. Whereas we have some excellent text-books on angling entomology, as yet we haven't filled that need for an angling entomological atlas, especially for still-water.

It takes some time to build up a picture of the 'insect' life of a fishery, and eager bug-hunters can help by compiling lists of fauna for the wall of the fishing hut. At Sundridge, in Kent, we located in our first year Corixa, Shrimp, Freshwater Louse, snails and various sizes and shapes, Lake Olive nymph and so forth. During that year sedges were rare, the following year plentiful. Imitations of these creatures, fished below the surface, were most successful, the specialists gradually building up an underwater map of ledges, weed-beds and other features where the fish hunted their natural prey.

This is the point where so many anglers give up, faced with the complexity of fishing the unseen areas with an imitation of what the trout may or may not be feeding on. There are some consolations. Firstly, from spooning out numerous trout, taken near to the bottom, preoccupied feeding seems less, and stomachs may frequently contain a mixture of many of the creatures already mentioned. And secondly, in deep water, where light is less intense, general representations trigger off the response by the fish. A brown nymph may well be accepted for a shrimp, hoglouse, caddis larva, alder larva, or many other things scuttling from place to place to escape the foraging hunter.

The mystery of the sunk line can then be simplified into the lure or fry attack, or else a simple range of nymphs of basic colours, brown, amber, white, black silver or gold. They will catch fish, as will standard wet flies, Butcher, Mallard & Claret, Greenwell, March Brown, fished in the same way. The extent to which you take this depends on yourself, either confined to this simple level, or taken to the stage of studying the books on angling entomology.

Referring back to the various types of sinking fly line, it becomes obvious that graduated depths can be searched in different ways. Fishing from the bank onto a ledge that slopes away, the sink-tip line, curving downwards from its floating belly, lifts a fly from the bottom towards the surface when the line is pulled with the left hand or rod tip. This is just like the beetle shooting skyward to renew his air supply, or the nymph, eager to burst from his shuck on the surface and to fly away as an adult.

In much deeper water the fast-sinking line drops down towards the bottom so that retrieved flies or lures move roughly parallel to the bottom. Sometimes the only indications of the fly being taken is a lift of the line between rod tip and water; at others a savage pull is distinctly felt. These are the mechanics of deep-water fishing, but the essential factor is to form a mental picture of the underwater terrain and how the trout searches for its food over the bottom plains.

Apart from tilting the thermal layers of deep water, the wind has a vital effect on trout activity. When quiet the surface film of the water is very strong, or 'sticky'. Insects from the land are trapped in this film and cannot easily free themselves. At such times they fall prey to cruising fish, on the look out for the Daddy Longlegs, the water-logged moth, the trapped flying ant or hawthorn fly. This is obvious enough, especially when these terrestrial creatures are in profusion. Less visible is the effect this 'stickiness' has on those nymphs and pupae struggling to break through the film to hatch into adults.

The Buzzer

The buzzer pupa is the most vulnerable of these, in calm, warm conditions being forced to hang immediately below the surface for quite long periods when it is most prolific. At such times literally thousands of these pupae will be in the same predicament – say on a summer's eve – and the trout will be cruising leisurely along, harvesting them with no expenditure of energy. The intelligent tactician now chooses the right fly and way to fish it to meet these conditions.

Firstly, the imitation is a problem, for the buzzer belongs to a varied family of non-stinging gnats, hatching from the water, and pupating from its larval form, the familiar water-butt bloodworm. The trouble is that they can vary enormously in size and colour. One lake may hold several varieties, though locally there will be a known pattern of the chief sizes and colours to interest the trout. The angler should know this, and tie these patterns for this contingency. Let's suppose there's an emergence of the large orange-silver buzzer, the colour of which is obvious from this name, and can be recognised either by seeing the adult in the air, the pupa in the water or crop of a recently taken fish.

The hook size is large, either 10 or 12, and orange silk is wound from round the bend of the hook towards the eye, ribbed with three or four turns of fine silver wire, then given a couple of coats of clear varnish or liquid plastic. A teased out fragment of orange wool is dubbed in just before the eye for the thorax, followed by a short piece of white floss silk, tied on top of the hook and left pointing forwards over the eye (these filaments copy the breathing tubes and perfectionists may add a further bunch as a tail). Finally a turn or two of peacock herl forms the head.

To fish this imitation right into the surface film, or immediately below it, requires some finesse. The leader is greased almost to the nymph which is cast so that it falls gently. We rarely achieve the target of having the nymph actually in the surface, unless a small collar of hackle or deer-hair is added to the neck of the fly. Normally the fly pierces the surface, goes down an inch or two and is then lifted towards the underside of the surface film by a gentle, short left-hand pull of line, ideally as the trout approaches.

Now suppose a breeze springs up suddenly. The conditions change. Immediately the fish are much harder to see if for no other reason than that the broken water conceals their surface activity. But there are other reasons. The molecular tension of the surface water is eased, and now pupae and nymphs shoot straight through the surface, hatching into adult flies speedily. The pace hots up, the trout moving faster from food item to item. Not only this, but as the water's surface is a confusion of broken points of light where small insects are hard to find and hit, trout frequently discover these creatures easier to hunt down some distance below the surface.

Normally under breezy conditions when flies, and buzzers or sedges especially, are still hatching, the slow sinking or sink-tip type lines may be more successful. It is in these strong winds when boat anglers learn that fish either miss altogether or come short to flies trailed close to the surface, whereas the imitations fished a yard or two lower in depth make solid contact.

The actual change of tactic is obviously a matter of judgement, the gentle ripple sometimes proving the most advantageous place of all to fish surface fly.

Small Lake Fisheries

There are two aspects of still-water fly-fishing which fall outside this general picture of the large expanses of water. There are the special problems of small lake fisheries, and the techniques of dry-fly fishing which have been unfairly discounted.

Small lake fisheries are usually commercial undertakings, developed to provide an income for the management. They may be worked-out gravel or sand pits; they may be special excavations fed by a small stream, or they may be settled lakes or ponds converted from coarse fish to trout. Their size gives certain advantages and drawbacks.

The main problem of a small-lake fishery is the rapid turnover in trout stock under rod pressure. If the entire year's supply of trout are introduced, say in March, by June the fish will be rather thin on the ground. The programme is geared to a continual topping up of stocks during the year, for which reason there are always large numbers of comparatively innocent fish waiting to be caught. The ratio of end-of-season survivors is probably lower than in a larger reservoir. Yet this accounts for the popularity of these pocket fisheries, and explains why the season permits on them command high prices. They represent the most extreme examples of put-and-take stocking policy.

This cannot be fairly criticised, for all trout fisheries contribute to easing the pressure on insufficient facilities, and to provide sport they must resort to this type of stocking policy. Management cannot provide for much, if any, growth rate when the fish survive so short a time, and consequently they are forced to buy a proportion of large fish with their general stocks. Frequently we read of specimen rainbows being caught in these fisheries, and I know that casual readers of angling papers believe these monsters have attained their weights by natural growth. This is rarely true. A rainbow of 8 lb. or so when caught was probably not far off that weight when introduced. The put-and-take fishery under heavy rod pressure allows even poor food-supply waters to provide 'instant sport', the rapid turnover in stock rendering natural food almost unimportant, while the paradox is that hungry trout will rise to the fly more freely, especially near to the surface.

On the other hand, the factor which makes fishing difficult is that small lakes swing violently through extremes of temperature, the more so as they are usually protected from cooling winds during long spells of summer heat. They may be prone to algae blooms of long duration, depriving the fishery of oxygen. In cold spells, the fishery also cools rapidly. These extremes of temperature may make fishing quite dour while they last.

The reservoir angler, when first switching to one of these small fisheries, may not appreciate that he is now close to his fish. The long line will rarely bring him an advantage, and in alarming trout close to his own position, it may even be counter-productive. He must learn to stalk fish carefully. He may no longer enjoy the same time margins as on large lakes, because small fisheries tend to become overpopulated during the day but are also affected by the changing temperature and light conditions. If rules allow it, the very early morning, when the lake is quiet, may well provide the best opportunity of all. Dusk is also productive, but on some lakes the dawn rise is invariably more productive than the evening rise when many anglers are afloat or on the banks, lining the fish.

If we now consider a very early morning at Sundridge lake as an example of the type of fishing that few anglers ever encounter, it will demonstrate the skill and reward of imitative fishing on the surface.

I arrive at the lake just after dawn in mid-summer, when light mists are veiling the calm surface. Here and there are dimpling rings as trout are sipping down small buzzers, or even caenis nymphs. I usually use a very light line on a limber, 10-ft. 'Bobfly' rod, for though I have to punch the line hard and tire my wrist, the fishing will be concentrated into a three-hour period, then home for breakfast. The leader is greased down to the last inch or two and a small 'Footballer' nymph is tied on – it's a fly I invented years ago when there seemed to be no effective copies of the natural – When all is ready, the punt is gently moved towards the main area of the rise and allowed to drift very gently. I now cast to every 'dimple' in sight and reach, sometimes being able to detect in which direction the fish is moving by the glimpse of a fin cleaving the surface film. The nymph pops through the film, and when the leader has settled the left hand gives the line the tiniest movement so that the leader leaves no wake at all. When the fish takes, I may see no more than the nylon pull down, or else where may be a definite swirl and hard tug. The tug is usually swift and sharp.

It would be wrong to imagine that these 'dimples' are all made by small fish. I am ready to flick the hook home, then immediately allow a large trout to run off line without fear of breakage by holding too firmly. The large rainbows will be mixed up with the small fish, and taking the rising pupae or nymph in the same fashion. The problem is that, using a very small imitation, the nylon point will be fine, but it's rare to encounter the 'smash take', even from large trout, in this sort of a rise, and the fireworks happen after the hook is home.

The sun starts to heave itself over the rim of the Weald, turning from a deep crimson to a brassy yellow which burns away the mists. By eight o'clock it's already hot enough to terminate this early morning rise, and usually the wind starts at this time. I could fish another hour or so, changing to a team of smallish wet flies, worked through the ripple. At this time, though, our first regular rods will arrive at the water, having missed the best of the day's fishing. They will still see odd fish rising in the ripple here and there, but many of these will be the leaping fish which rarely take a fly, exciting though they are to watch. Later still, even this ceases, and the boring business of plugging away with the sunken line takes over in the exhausting heat of the day. It succeeds from time to time, due to the great depths at Sundridge.

In the evening I may return. I give myself an hour to explore the water, sometimes by walking round the lake to see where the clouds of adult buzzers are hovering, for from this area fertile females will be returning to the water to lay eggs, while obviously they all hatched from a nearby bed of larvae. A few sedges near the bushes will tell me to expect activity in that vicinity. Failing this, by scanning the lake through pocket binoculars I look for swooping martens or rising trout. Frequently I'm able to choose an area where trout will be active as the sun falls.

Three obvious things happen: the light intensity declines, the wind usually dies down and the air cools. On still-water insect activity now is based on the buzzer, hatching and egg-laying; and the sedges. The latter are easy to see, for sedge rises are usually hectic, the former guessed at mainly by the leisurely, cruising rise of the fish below the surface.

The fishing is similar to that of early morning, though the rise is sometimes different in form, in the evening being generally more prominent. Plumping either for the buzzer nymph or else the dry or wet sedge fly, my aim is still to cover the fish I see, and the more I fish in this way the more easily I can detect in which direction and depth a fish is going and where to intercept him with the fly. In the end I can almost tell myself when the fish is going to take, or if I have made some slight error in speed or direction of cast to miss him altogether. An elementary example of this is that when my line is already in the air I drop the fly quite close to the edge of the circle of the rise, whereas if I'm already fishing in another direction, and I have first to lift off, pick up line speed for the cast and then shoot for him, I have to allow perhaps a yard or two for the time lapse. It would be futile to put my fly where the fish had just been!

For the imitative fly fisherman I've discussed here techniques which should cover about 80% of his surface fishing on still-water, for while lakes and reservoirs produce a wide variety of insect life, the buzzer and sedge account for most of it. This is a good stage to talk about the fly patterns to use.

For the buzzer pupa, the simple Footballer should suffice. The standard pattern has alternate bands of black and white horsehair wound up the body side by side from round the hook bend. This is followed by a smallish knob of mole's fur for the thorax and a few turns of peacock herl for the head. This fly has accounted for thousands of trout during a rise to the buzzer pupa, irrespective of size and colour. It can be sophisticated easily by making the body of various colours, covered with clear nylon, and matching dubbings of fluorescent wool.

When trout are taking the hatching sedge I've found no better fly than the standard Invicta, fished just below the surface. It works well when the wings and hackles are clipped short so that the fly can be fished right in the surface film, and by using stiff hackles it also makes a killing dry fly. The Amber Nymph is an alternative, while some tyers make the Invicta with either green or brown bodies as alternatives, according to the colour of their local caddis population. It goes without saying that sedges and buzzers vary in size and colour from lake to lake and it makes sense to dress your own imitations accordingly.

I've confined myself to rather 'purist' methods for small lakes. We always start these fisheries with noblest thoughts in mind, and if we were able to restrict them to ourselves and like-minded friends, this would be sufficient. As soon as we let out rods, then pressure starts to allow for lures, fry imitations, wet-fly teams and so forth. The facts of life are that I've known no one able to resist this pressure for long, myself included. The small lake methods I've described apply to reservoirs, and reservoir methods overlap onto the pocket fisheries. If you can tow a lure about a reservoir, you can drag it as easily through a smaller lake, so there's no need to discuss it further here.

Dry Fly on Still Water

Tactically speaking, there's a choice between the 'wake fly' and the dry fly proper. The former is a searching method for fish, which are attracted to the surface by the furrow of a large dry fly being worked back to the boat or bank. Such a fly as a large moth or Muddler Minnow can be fished at random even when there's no surface rise in progress. It is effective on a summer's evening when the wake fly is fished either with floating line or shooting head. Trout often hunt the tree-lined margins for moths which fall into the water at dusk, the struggles of which spread out the rings of panic across the water. The shallows where dam-walls slide into the water are other such hunting grounds, and, rules permitting, at dusk it's a good strategy to drag a wake fly along the surface, parallel and close to the dam.

Dapping can be likened to wake-fly fishing in that the aim is to make a surface commotion by dibbling a large dry fly onto the surface, though this is done from a drifting boat with a long rod, even up to 16 ft., and a special blow-line made from floss silk. The rod is held high and the wind carries this light line in front of the craft. The fly is attached to a normal leader, and the art is to bounce the artificial or natural insect on the wavelets. The Crane fly, or Daddy Longlegs, and the Mayfly are the usual ammunition for this tactic.

Large limestone loughs in Ireland have their recognised dapping seasons, the 'Greendrake' fortnight for the mayfly, the 'daddy season' towards autumn, but on English reservoirs you should check the rules before using the method, especially if you intend to impale the natural flies onto your hook. I evolved an adaptation of the normal 10-ft. Bobfly boat-rod for occasional dapping simply by tying in a 'butterfly' of cigarette paper about a yard up the leader, which will be carried out by a moderate breeze even when using a normal size 6 fly line. I've made some goodish catches with this idea, using artificial mayflies and daddies.

One final point on dapping is that trout tend to find a way of submerging the fly, sometimes with tail smashes, sometimes by seizing it only with their lips at first. It pays to watch carefully before striking, making sure the fish really has taken the fly firmly.

What about the true dry fly? Why has it been so unpopular on lakes?

The truth is that the still-water fisherman has been educated not so much in favour of the wet fly or lure as in the philosophy of the active retrieve. He feels as if he must be doing something to attract the fish. The concept of watching an inert dry fly is foreign to him. Actually a dry fly is rarely inert, wind and water movement see to that. This explains why dry fly has only recently been investigated for lake fishing. Iven's first book, for all its worth, condemned it, and although I tried myself to redress the balance by the first edition of *Fly-Fishing Tactics on Still Water* as early as 1968, it wasn't until two angling entomologists, John Goddard and C. F. Walker, made the first close studies of still-water fly life that interest developed, mainly on the smaller fisheries but also on the larger English reservoirs.

There are formidable physical problems, outlined earlier, explaining how difficult it is to determine from one rise where the fish will be by the time you're ready to cast your fly. In fairness, when trout are actually taking floating insects it is often because there are so many of them on the surface already, and the fish move less quickly than they do during a scattered appearance of larvae or pupae. Also, when the insects are large, as with sedge flies for instance, you may well be able to see the nearest fly to the last rise, and guess the fish is on its way there.

I experienced a typical instance of this some few years ago at Chew lake, in Somerset, when in the evening I saw a row of four sedges on the surface, the first of which was knocked off by a trout. I sat my fly down on the end of the queue and caught the angry rainbow who was munching his way along . . . 'the intestine rules of world', as the famous French entomologist, Fabre, so properly remarked.

This dry-fly fishing, then, imposes the problem of making rapid switches in distance and direction. If you see a trout hit a sedge some twenty yards in front of you, you push out a long line, letting the fly settle in advance of its estimated direction. If nothing happens, and suddenly another fish rises twelve yards to your left, you have to make the necessary adjustment to your next cast, and make it quickly enough to cover the fish before it moves too far, increasing the possible angle of error with every yard it travels until it is beyond the area of vision from your fly.

The equipment for this type of fishing is a light dry-fly rod, say equivalent to a 'Two Lakes', with fastish action. The normal double-taper floating line is by far the most versatile because, unlike other types of line and shooting heads, it can be rolled off the water. If you can visualise again the change in distance and direction I've just mentioned, you may see that the fly, at twenty yards distance, has to be switched to twelve yards in a new direction. The line had to 'lose' some eight yards quickly. If you merely pulled this line back through the rings, the fly would become waterlogged, your opportunity lost. The very first act is to get that fly into the air by making a roll-cast, smartly snapping the rod downwards from behind the shoulder to bowl a loop along the line, as shown in the illustration in the casting chapter.

As this loop reaches the fly it hoists it off the water, when a vigorous left-hand haul of line starts you into the first false-cast needed to measure the change of direction and length of line.

As the life-cycles of insects follow a seasonal progression on rivers, so do they on lakes. The whole story is too varied and complex to reproduce here, but there are a number of specialised books available for further study. Lakes have their sedges, most of which resemble each other well enough for three patterns of dry fly to suffice, the Cinnamon Sedge, the Small Red Sedge and the Dark Sedge for the so-called Silverhorn hatch. A few waters glory in a huge sedge fly called the Murragh, for which a red sedge pattern on a size 6 or 8 hook is effective.

The buzzers dominate most lakes, and their life history has already been related. The angler must discover for himself the prevalent size and colour of buzzer on his favourite lakes from which copies can be made. The Ephermeridae are represented mainly by the Lake or Pond Olives, very similar to the Medium Olives of running water. The Greenwell's Glory is a good copy. We encounter mayflies on still-water rarely in England, one exception being on the picturesque Clatworthy reservoir in Devon, but on the Irish limestone lakes they are prolific in their season. Here and there we bump into rarer species of Ephemeridae, the Sepia and Claret Duns, for instance, and having found out their locality, the reference books cite effective patterns for them. The tiny Caenis is everywhere, the dry Grey Duster being my own favourite dry fly, for the arrival of this 'Angler's Curse', cursed for its minute size that is.

9 Migratory Fish

Every fly-fisherman is aware that his sport is crowded with paradoxes. One of these is that although the game has this tremendous diversification between delicate dry fly at one end of the scale and the hefty sunk salmon fly at the other, there's also a unity of method in casting, working the fly, striking and playing the fish which allows the specialist to adapt rapidly to another branch of fly-fishing. The hard truth about salmon fishing is that it's fairly simple, involving none of the finesse of approaching, say, a wary brown trout in a clear-water stream. The main problem of the salmon is whether or not he's in a 'taking' mood.

No one can be certain that the salmon is unalarmed by the presence of people. On occasion I've made some clumsy move while dry-fly fishing on the Test, emptying the pool of trout and grayling, only to discover the resident salmon was calmly holding his place in the current when his neighbours bolted for cover. Many is the time I've seen a salmon suddenly come to a fly or spoon after being 'lined' several times by careless casters. I've also fished for and taken salmon on pools where the limitations of space forced the fish and myself to be in full view of each other. This doesn't mean that one should discard all the usual rules of caution. If the fish rarely shows his feelings, that scarcely implies he doesn't have any.

In salmon fishing we are usually blessed with the knowledge of exactly where the fish will be at any given height of water. For generations the fish have occupied the same pools and those who own or watch the water know these places well. The same knowledge also gives exact directions as to which position to cast from to present the fly to the salmon in those lies. These are tremendous short cuts in contrast to working up a trout stream, looking for your targets, then planning your attack. Very often, on a salmon beat you will have a ghillie, who says to you in effect: 'The fish lies there. You stand here and cast your fly to that point . . .'

I've never cared for this tradition, probably because I was reared on trout streams. I prefer either to rent a stretch of river or fish an Association water where I can find my own fish, fish for them my own way and land them without help.

Once I rented a tumbledown thatched cottage on the River Blackwater in

Ireland, some six miles from Fermoy. Here I was thrown in at the deep end, for the only information given to me was the limits of the beat below, and the very first task was to spend some considerable time in prospecting the water to find out where the salmon lay. To me, this is part of the sport. Not being a regular salmon fisherman in the sense that I have continual access to a river, I've built up some rough and ready rules to suit my occasional forays to favourite rivers. One of these is to watch the river early in the morning, and again at dusk, when the fish are more inclined to reveal their presence by leaping or rolling. Then I mark these places by pushing sticks into the bank in line with the appearance of the fish.

On the Blackwater I was lucky enough to have a vantage point on the brow of a hill which overlooked the entire stretch, and salmon, being hefty fish, can be seen from even a few hundred yards away. On a twisty river, like some parts of the Torridge, the first thing is to find the sort of places likely to hold salmon, then watch these in succession. As a matter of curiosity I checked a number of popular books on salmon fishing to discover information about the requirements of a 'holding' pool. Opinions were sparse, probably because on such-and-such a river these pools are well known, and that is sufficient. The reasons why the salmon stay in them is unimportant.

These pools are resting places between surges up through the strong currents and obviously the salmon doesn't want to burn up energy simply to remain still. I watched a pair of resting salmon for a whole morning on the river Cothi. Apparently they were lying in fastish water, until a closer look at the pool showed a rocky ledge deflecting the full force of the current away from them. Above these fish were some four feet of water, below a flat bed of rock. It becomes apparent that when the water level rises these fish would run, but places not deep enough at low summer levels can hold fish when more water is flowing between the banks.

These two fish were lying in this pool at the lower summer level. The ledge deflected the full force of the current from them, yet they were not lying in slack water. They were enjoying a moderate flow spilling through the pool. The surface flow of a pool can thus be deceptive, for below there may be ledges and ridges to break the full force of the current. In truth, one renowned pool on the lower Torridge is called 'the Ledges' for this very reason. I remember, too, a quite shallow run on another part of the Torridge in the middle of which was a large boulder. The current had scoured out a deepish hole behind the big rock and almost invariably a salmon would be lying in it.

Simply by watching fish an idea of where to find their neighbours is built up, for already we know that in summer the salmon will prefer deepish water with moderate flow, especially where this is afforded by some protective obstacles in fastish pools . . . reasonable depth, moderate flow, these can truly be said to be the keys to finding the fish.

Sunk Fly or Greased Line

In Britain we normally fish for the salmon with a simple wet-fly technique. When the water is cold the fly is sunk deep at a fairly narrow angle downstream. It was for this method in the old days that the really large flies were

Gaffing a salmon on the
Dorset Stour, Christchurch

made, and consequently the long, powerful two-handed rods. This has been changed by use of modern fast-sinking or high-density lines, enabling us to fish a fairly small fly deeply, and even allowing for a wider angle of casting. Nevertheless, if one part of salmon fly-fishing has given way to spinning, it is the sunk fly, especially in the spring when water levels are usually higher than the special markers that some Associations use to determine when spinning can be allowed. On my last visit to the Border Esk, although the level was suited to fly-fishing I was the only angler among many who was using fly gear.

When the water is warm the fish take just below the surface. The dividing line is generally accepted as a water temperature of 50° F. Then we use floating lines and light, thinly dressed flies, the 'low water' patterns. The technique is again quite straightforward, the fly being cast across the current so that it passes over the head of the fish, yet below the surface without skating. The only problem here is that it may be necessary to mend the line during the progress of the fly to avoid skittering it on the surface. Books have been written on these two methods, but during the last two years my interest has been aroused by two little-used techniques, the dry-fly and the nymph. What seems to have happened in Britain is that fly-fishing for salmon has become frozen into these two wet-fly methods, mostly with old-fashioned conceptions in tackle.

But let's leave the traditional methods of fly-fishing in their basic simplicity and discuss further the nymph and the dry fly. The success of the nymph on Avon salmon was proved by Frank Sawyer some years ago. As for the dry-fly, I know there are some places, such as the Isle of Lewis, where it enjoys local success. In Mayfly time on the Test I have been smashed all over the place by an unsought salmon suddenly lunging at a floating Drake intended for a nearby rainbow. I caught a grilse on the Torridge when fishing a dry Royal Coachman for sea-trout. Reports have been given of American anglers successfully using their dry-fly methods on Scottish rivers. Finally, I know, too, that one fine Irish angler, the late 'Lemon Grey', used to go after 'potted', red salmon that had long grown stale in the river with a green nymph fished almost directly upstream to them.

As expressed earlier, I see no reason why we shouldn't enjoy a revolution in fly-fishing styles for salmon, in using lighter, single-handed rods, which in North America facilitated the development of dry-fly and nymph methods. Certainly during these last two years, when salmon fishing has recovered patchily from the mortal disease U.D.N., I have visited Welsh and West Country rivers with single-handed rods, one loaded with a size 6 line for light work, the other with a size 8 Forward Taper for the bigger pools, such as one meets on the lower Towy. Admittedly this may be too short a time to guarantee conclusive results, but already some conclusions may be drawn.

New Methods

The first thing is that upstream nymph and dry fly do work. Secondly, they offer a better chance of taking fish under the trying conditions we've experienced in, for example, the summers of '72 and '73 when week after week passed by with no rain, the rivers falling to low levels of very clear water. Anglers living near to salmon rivers can afford to wait their moment, but those who have to plan their fishing trips in advance should know that as long as there are fish in the pools there is a chance of catching them with these unorthodox methods.

Until now I've concluded that the colour of flies fished on or close to the surface is relatively unimportant. Simple dark or light colours suffice for the dry fly, the former being useful in clear light, the latter when it's diffused or growing dark. A plain black Palmer with silver rib, heavily dressed on low-water hooks, is very effective for straightforward floating techniques on rivers, or for deliberately whiffling on lakes or lochs. A white-and-silver version provides the light-coloured fly.

For a specialised dry fly that has killed well in Canada, I'm indebted to the American expert Joe Bates, who suggested I might try the 'Bottlewasher'. Joe quotes the inventor, Francois Gourdeau, as saying, 'I fish this dry fly upstream with four or five casts directly in front of the fish, leaving the fly on the surface for about two seconds. It usually doesn't take long before the fish gets mad and goes for it.'

The fly is tied on large, fine-wire hooks, from $1\frac{1}{2}$ in. to 2 in. long. The tag is divided into two sections, the back half of black wool, the front half of yellow wool, occupying about a quarter of the length of the shank. The rest of the body is a heavily dressed brown Palmer, tapering towards the tail.

When it comes to describing 'nymphs' we obviously cannot think in imitative terms. The word 'Nymph' describes in this context a fly which is fished upstream, and comes down to the salmon virtually inert, save for the play of the hackles in the water. The pattern I've come across time and time again, both in catching salmon deliberately or by accident, is Iven's Green Nymph, the body of which is made by winding green nylon over an underbody of white floss silk. The hackle is of brown partridge and the head is a few turns of peacock herl. Experimentation has been going on with this same structure, but in brightening the body by using coloured tinsels and fluorescent wool tags.

Let me recall here the time I first connected with a salmon on the dry fly. I had gone to the upper reaches of the Torridge, only to discover low, bright water and a few stale fish trapped in the pools. It was either a choice to go all the way to fish in the sea or to graft away at these reddish salmon and the peal. I chose the latter. On the elbow of a pool I spotted a fish, thought to be a sea trout, sniffing at the surface. I had a dry Royal Coachman on the leader, which I floated down the pool two or three times. The salmon took the fly by rolling over onto it, diving down and hooking itself. It struck me then that there's no reason to desert the river when these arid conditions persist.

The thing that could change our salmon fishing ideas most quickly would be the diversification by our still-water specialists. Most fly-fishermen in Britain today are forced to start on the banks of the nearest trout reservoirs. I wish they would take their tackle with them when they go on holiday, and, being unfearful of the traditions, put their single-handed rods to good use on the rivers they find, with their own nymphs, lures and dry flies. This could bring about the rationalisation of salmon fishing tackle and methods similar to that of North America, for logic tells us that there's no reason why the same species of fish should succumb to nymph and dry fly as near as Iceland, yet be selective to the sunk and low-water fly only in Britain.

The other American innovation, which I confess to lacking the courage to try, is deliberately to skitter the fly across the water. After the fly is tied onto the leader, a further half-hitch is made round the head of the fly so that it will drag at an angle to the current, either on the surface or below it according to choice. The only hint that this might work occasionally in Britain was given to me on the Test when a resting salmon charged a dry Mayfly, just as I was skimming it back on the surface for another cast.

Now, having whetted your appetite for experimentation, allow me to conclude with the standard information on which most 'occasional' salmon anglers rely, for one thing can be said about the salmon – 'it is a stable fish', and, as we've already observed, to the competent fly-fisherman the only problem is whether or not he's in a 'taking' mood. Some complex theories have been advanced on this problem, and those wishing to take it further could hardly do better than read Reg Rhygini's fine study on the subject, entitled *Salmon Taking Times,* to which may be added what is probably the best text book on salmon fly-fishing, Balfour-Kinnear's *Flying Salmon.*

'Taking' Salmon

At my level of occasional salmon fever I work to the rule that a fresh-run fish is more likely to take the fly than a stale one, simply because I believe the salmon fly is accepted as an item of colourful marine plankton. The longer the fish rests in fresh water so does this conditioning factor wear off. I think every salmon angler longs to be attacking the fish which have recently entered a pool on a spate, and rest there as the water starts to fall and clear itself of silt. These are obviously advantages to the man who has continual access to the river.

Apart from this I have a personal preference for interposing my fly between the fish and the source of light, the sun, whether bright in a clear sky or hidden by cloud, for I think that salmon are visually conscious of the sun even when hidden to our eyes. The largest fish I hooked was spotted by myself when fishing the Border Esk, near to Canonbie. There having been a spate the day before, the popular pools like 'the Willows' and 'the Cauldron' were crowded by long ranks of anglers, spinning. I knew of a small hole further upstream called the 'Burn Pool' which held only a fish or two when water levels were higher than normal, and on my way upstream to Canonbie I saw the fresh-silver of a spring-run fish.

I reckoned then that if I fished three pools above me, down through the town, by the time I returned to the pool the sun, though hidden behind snow clouds, would be silhouetting my fly from the salmon's position. So it was that at four in the afternoon, in flurries of snow, though with a faint, brassy glow across the pool, I brought my hair-wing Thunder & Lightning across the current to be trapped by the light. On the second swing round of the fly, he had it! Of course I cannot prove this theory, but it gives me confidence to so arrange an attack with conditions favouring my tactics, even if it only keys up the expectation.

Two styles of salmon fly: Thunder and Lightning Hair Wing, for spring and back-end fishing, and a Low Water for summer and greased line

I think it largely true that the pattern of the fly is less important than its size. Many a time a fish will come to fly, then turn away short, only to be caught on the next cast with a smaller fly. It's especially true that the size of the low-water fly may well need to be changed, not only from pool to pool but at different parts of the same pool, to fish it properly just below the surface without skating, interposed nicely between the fish and the mirror-like sky above.

In former times the size of the fly was determined by how deep it would fish at various speeds on an undressed silk line in cold water, or a greased line in warm water. Today the choice of lines is wider and the performance of them decides the depth for us, and allows us to fish with much smaller flies, the logic of which should lead to the wider use of the lighter, single-handed rod. My preference is to start with the smallest size of fly, determining the depth with the type of line, from fast-sinking lines in cold-water or swollen, coloured flows, down to the floating line with lightly dressed flies in low, bright conditions of summer. The floating lines with sinking tips are first-class, especially for normal levels, when a fly can be fished at the point of a long leader to

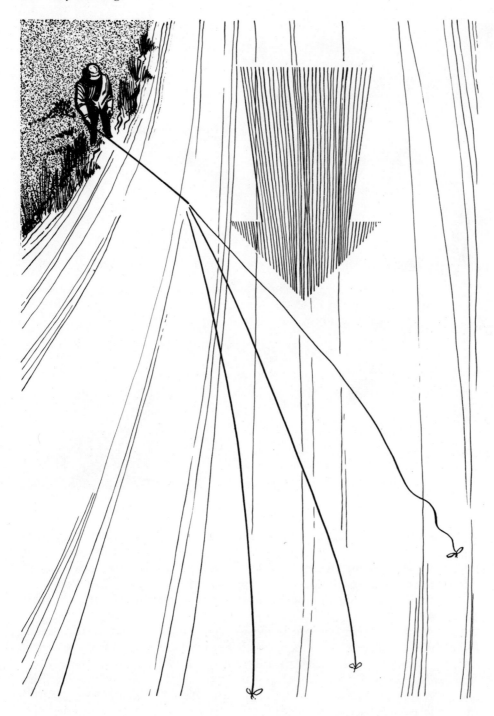

Fishing a deeply sunk fly at a
sharp angle downstream

search out the depths, while a smaller, light fly may be fished very high up the
leader to see if the salmon want to 'come up'.

Choice of flies are limited to three types: for sunlight, a gay pattern with a

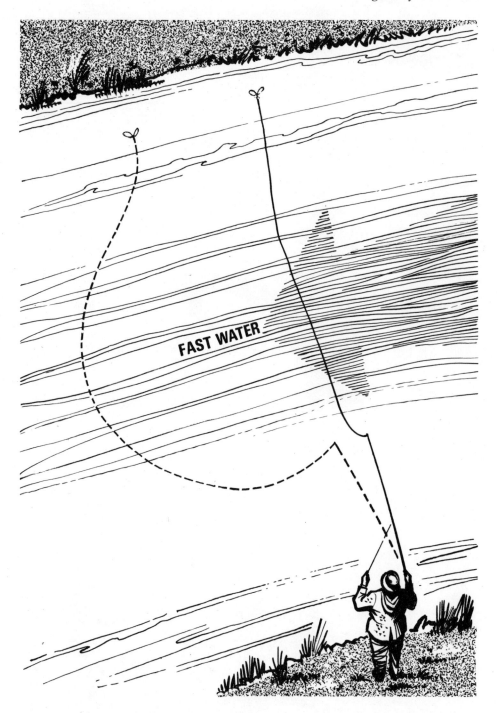

FAST WATER

Current bellying line

tinselled body, my two favourites being the Torrish and Mar Lodge. For water with some colour, I use a coloured fly such as the Green Highlander or Jock Scott (notice how frequently the latter's combination of black-and-yellow

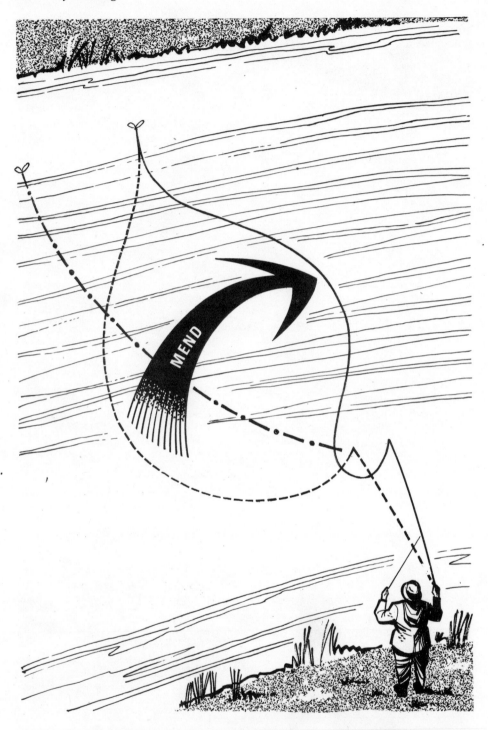

Making an upstream mend
of the line

body colour crops up in other patterns). For 'silhouette' fishing as described above, I use dullish flies with lots of tentacle-like mobility, patterns like the Spey Lady Caroline or Grey Heron, and my favourite hair-wing Thunder &

Lightning. Most of these patterns can be tied up as Low Water flies, on tubes of varying weights and as normal fully-dressed flies on ordinary forged hooks.

The angle of the attack is governed by the speed of the water and by tradition. The big flows have to be fished with a long line downstream, while in summer we use a floating line across, even up and across the current, with line-mending to avoid drag. Most anglers work down a salmon pool, and this may be compulsory on Association waters, where after spates you often have to join the queue. Where some privacy is enjoyed, not only should you fish back up the pool, even starting from the tail, but the practice of casting up above the fish from a position downstream of it has born fruit. The first time I found this being recommended was in Lemon Grey's 'Torridge Fishery', one of the top three books on salmon in my view.

Timing the Strike

Having described striking and playing fish in a general way in an earlier chapter, I should add that the salmon doesn't reject the fly as quickly as the trout realises its mistake, and my recommendation for the strike to be a nice, steady pull should hook the fish well. Fresh fish usually rush upstream against pressure – but not always, for I was eventually broken by a large Springer that decided to head back to the oceans. The trout man tends to make a fast snatchy strike at a salmon, but if he can steel himself he should remember that with the salmon you always have time, time to let the line tighten as the fish moves away to his lie, fly in mouth.

Never having used a ghillie, where I can beach a fish I will. In deeper places I use the net, and I never use a gaff. I'm a great believer in 'walking' a fish, but only when he starts to turn onto his flank in weariness. 'Walking' simply means clamping the reel drum firmly, and, not holding the rod too high, you walk either backwards to bring the fish to your bank, or upstream to bring him to a less dangerous reach. On those lucky times when fish bolt fast upstream, a habit of summer grilse, when they run out of steam, you'll find that coaxing them back, head downstream again is usually sufficient to drown them or knock the stuffing out of them.

The preceding pages are intended to give a reliable guide to occasional visitors to salmon rivers, perhaps to still-water men wishing to widen their experience. They should take heart, there's no difficulty for a competent caster in salmon-fly work, and nowadays our lighter, single-handed reservoir rods will fish the fly and kill the fish in most rivers in Britain, no matter what the dyed-in-the-wool traditionalist may say.

Breaking the rules with Sea-Trout

As with the salmon, let me tell you about something completely new, something forced on my by circumstance. One autumn I booked a few days for salmon on the Cothi, a tributary of the Towy, which normally holds a good head of fish, even in the long drought we were enduring at that particular time. True, the three-quarters of a mile I fished did have fish, some fourteen salmon, all of which were in various stages of the U.D.N. disease. My companions and I decided to cut short our visit, but first I had the chance of one night's fishing.

During the late afternoon I made another reconnaissance of the beat, this time looking for sea-trout which usually occupy different types of water to salmon. I was searching now the tails of long, gravelly runs. All told, in the entire length there were two small schools of sewin and my friend and I decided to take one each after dark, my own pool having a mere six fish. Next, I took one long, hard look at the pool and my spirits began to ebb. There was just no way to fish for them from above, for the nearest entry point was some fifty yards above them with the pool sulking under a tunnel of dark-green trees. I had an instinctive feeling that these fish would not move up at dusk, they looked so sullen and unmoving, hugging the very bottom of the run.

Below the pool was a fastish stickle from which I could wade to my wader tops into the bottom of the pool, leaving a cast of some eighteen yards. I marked the position to drop the fly under an overhanging branch, all in all a murderous combination for night fishing. My friends on the Torridge would never cast until they could count seven stars twinkling in the firmament, but as I reached my position I knew I should never even see the sky, so dense was the foliage above me, sprouting from steep banks of the Cothi gorge.

It soon grew very dark indeed, black as your hat, but just before the light died away I saw the faintest sign of a rolling of the surface water beneath the branch. At least the fish were on the fin. My strategy was to make a long cast directly upstream with a size 6 Teal, Blue and Silver, which I would strip back above the fish, hoping the darkness would conceal wake of leader. Trouble was I couldn't see a damn thing, nor even the light-coloured floating line. I also had to unroll the line in a very narrow loop under the trees, and believe me, I began to feel very forlorn indeed with only owl-hoots and the chuckle of the water for company.

Summoning up my courage, I made the cast, felt the fly hit the water some-where up there, under the tree, and I began to strip back. Suddenly the line tightened, sang away, and a two-pounder was scattering glistening drops of water to the left of the pool where a solitary moonbeam had sneaked through a gap in the leaves. It was the only 'take' that night, the other fish bolting up the pool in alarm as I played out my solitary victim.

I've never heard or read advice to fish a wet fly straight upstream at night for sea-trout, for the problems are formidable. It's hard to keep in touch with the fly as it tumbles back downstream. How can you avoid lining the fish, for darkness makes all casting a matter of 'feel'? And should you strip too fast the wake may well put down the fish. Here I was governed by necessity, having come a long way and paid good money, only to find sick salmon, with very few sewin left in the runs. I had one ghost of a chance, and I took it. Nor would I normally recommend night fishing in the Cothi, it's an extremely dangerous river, besides being the haunt of poacher gang and poison bottle.

Finding the Fish

Let's have a look at the lessons gleaned from this bizarre experience. First of all, sea-trout don't always lie in the same places as salmon, for I counted the diseased fish on my first expedition along the stretch. It took a second trip to discover if any sea-trout were at home. They like long pools of easy water, and during the daylight hours usually lie inert at the bottom, which they prefer to be smooth and even. They may be found by day in the tails of pools, or under deeply-cut banks on the 'far side' of pools, but by night, if they move, it will often be into quieter water. 'If they move . . .' that's the sixty-four dollar question, for writers usually assume they will move at dusk into smoother glides above or below their daylight haunts. It's truer to say that they may move to these places, but sometimes they remain where they are, perhaps becoming more active in darkness, moving to your fly and natural food. The reasons for this remain obscure, though I've noticed a disinclination to change position at dusk when the river is small, or heavily fished by day, especially with the spinning rod and spoon.

The lone angler is frequently forced to make vital decisions, none being more vital than the choice of his fishing station at night. Where banks are open, his best bet is to station himself at the tail of the pool as dusk falls, watching for signs of fish movement, for sea-trout will nearly always 'show' at last light. The rolling, surface-breaking or actual leap clear of the water will prove whether they are remaining in their day-time 'lies' or if they will travel to the heads or tails of the runs.

Although I was forced to fish upstream, finding it difficult to keep in touch with the fly as it was brought back on a slack line by the current, the main aim of night fishing is to keep the line as straight as possible, which means fishing across and down the current, 'keeping in touch with the fly', a phrase that crops up all the time in wet-fly fishing downstream. What does it mean? Taken literally, you should actually feel the fly working in the current, like a live thing on the end of your line.

Referring back to this 'unity' in fly-fishing methods, it matters little if you're fishing across the current for ordinary trout, mighty salmon, sea-trout or humble grayling, the action is the same. As soon as the line falls across the flow, dropping the fly across the stream, the current immediately takes hold of the line, pushing a belly into the middle part of it so that the fly on the end is suddenly speeded up in its progress downstream. Being tethered to the leader, it isn't free to be washed away by this force and is made to swing round below you. If this force is too fierce, the fly is also pushed onto the surface of the water, causing it to 'skate'.

Your intention should be to control this speed so that the fly swings round at the depth you choose, at a reasonable speed. At night, it will skim across the nose of the sea-trout, who will come after it from his lie. If the fly isn't seized during its faster travel, it eventually winds up directly below you, motionless in the stream, or 'on the dangle' as it's termed. You than work the fly back towards you by left-hand retrieve of line, a time also in which a following fish may snatch it.

One thing is certain, in wet-fly fishing, by day or night, words help but little.

The subtle techniques involving depths, speed and retrieve are achieved only by experience, for no two pools are alike. Imagine a piece of water, just below a very fast stickle: even though the river-bed is falling away towards a slow pool, at this point the power of the current is so strong that almost immediately after your first cast across the river you will have to throw an upstream loop, or 'mend', to slow down the fly. The current needs more time to straighten, and then to bend downstream your line, during which pause the fly will sink and swing round relatively smoothly.

The exact opposite of this is the deep, sluggishly flowing pool, where not only will you have to lead the line downstream with the rod-tip, but you may well have to add some life to the fly by retrieving the line in your left hand. Between these two extremes are all varieties of pool where gentle adjustments need to be made to add or decrease speed to the line and fly to give it naturally attractive motion. Only experience of the river can yield knowledge to these rough guidelines.

Speed apart, the depth at which the fly fishes is another related factor, made easier today by choice of types of fly-line, as described earlier. At night you have to make the next decision, to fish the fly relatively high in the water or close to the bottom. The floating line holds the fly high in normal water, though in fast runs the sink-tip type may be needed to prevent the fly from skating. Sinking lines take the fly deep, slow-sinking lines in quieter pools, medium or even fast-sinking lines for torrents.

In salmon fishing, the choice between low-water flies and heavy patterns is decided by water and air temperature, for when the former exceeds the latter salmon are said to 'come up' to the fly. The same is true of sea-trout, but as so few of us would trouble to take comparison temperatures we content ourselves with fishing the fly high in the water when the water and air together are warm, as on overcast evenings. On clear, cold nights we may well choose to fish the fly nearer to the bottom.

It's true that this type of fishing is straightforward wet-fly work, with the added complication of darkness. It's equally true that, before night fishing for sea-trout is attempted, it should follow a fair amount of normal wet-fly fishing for trout and grayling in daylight, the great teacher of which is the river herself, for gradually this mysterious 'feel' will develop, of how the line and fly react to the various speeds and depths of pool, and what you should do to take advantage of these conditions.

The problem is that the very first time you apply this by night, that 'feel' vanishes. The timing of the casting goes to pot, the line falls heavily on the surface and distance is impossible to gauge. Here are some rules for night-fishing:

1. Although the darkest nights are best, to start with choose bright nights and rivers with open banks.
2. Choose light-coloured lines, measure your distances by daylight on the pools, marking your line with a thread you can feel between your fingers where it leaves the reel. This ensures correct distance. Even so, fish the shortest pools first.
3. Go with an experienced companion, but give him elbow room. Don't chatter or call to him during the night.

4. Fish for short periods at first, and if nothing happens in the first two hours, go home.
5. Cast across the river, keeping the line against your sensitive forefinger until you learn what the fly does to the line as it settles through the surface, swings down and ends up on the dangle.
6. Strike any gentle 'take', but not too savagely as sea-trout have soft mouths. In spite of their tendency to leap and double back, try to play them sweetly to avoid scaring the remaining fish in the school. Use a white-painted rim on your landing net to guide your fish to the bank.
7. Use a long, soft rod to keep the line high over bushes behind you. It's fatal to stumble about in the water or on the bank when tangled.
8. If hopelessly snagged, break off the leader. It's easier to change leaders than flies at night. Don't use a torch unless you have to, then mask its light from the river.
9. Keep to a single, large fly of simple pattern. Three types suffice for night fishing: silver-bodied for moonlight, yellow-bodied for medium light and a black fly for the darkest nights. Teal Blue & Silver, Invicta and Connemara Black on size 6, are very reliable. They're big enough to 'feel'.

To this must be added the warning, 'know your river'. If you're a visitor, go down to the pool in daylight, mark wading limits and entry points with white sticks. Remember, above all, the wariness of the quarry. A pool can be ruined for the night by steel wader-hobs grating on shingle, or by prodding wading sticks into the bed of the river.

Sea-trout and salmon both return from the sea to the rivers for spawning, but unlike the salmon the sea-trout feeds in fresh-water, especially by night. It chases sedges, nymphs and small fish with eagerness once its natural wariness is overcome. They can be caught by day on fly and spinner, and in rivers as well as the lakes into which they run. The larger sea-trout, sometimes well into 'teens of pounds, tend to run with the big spring salmon, and are caught in similar fashion. The smaller school-fish come into the rivers in late spring and summer, with a sprinkling of larger fish with them. These are the fish with definite ideas on residence, the ones I prefer to catch at night, not only because bigger bags can be made in darkness when the fish lose something of their shyness but because this sport has a particular fascination of its own.

I often start to fish at night with a sense of hopelessness, which I rarely feel by day. It seems so unlikely that a glide, seen to be empty of fish by day, would hold any by night. The line swings round below me, then there's a feeble pluck as if a dead leaf had lodged on the hook, and yet, as I tighten, the line sings away, the pool below explodes into a silvery sheen of splintered fragments, while I vaguely try to tranquilise the angry opponent. There's the problem of knowing where he's bolting to, of playing him gently while preventing the pool from being too grossly disturbed. The fish may well be two pounds or so. On good nights others will follow. Then, once in a while, the line will tighten into an opponent, heroic and relentless in his fight. If I win, he may go ten pounds or more, and if not there's just the dismay of losing when the odds are stacked against me in the darkness of the night.

10 'The Lady of the Stream'

The grayling is unique, being a member of the salmonidae family, as we call our game fish, and yet sharing its spawning months with the coarse fish. It has a huge dorsal fin with 19 to 22 rays, a feature which is brought home when playing one of these streamlined fish against the current. No one could mistake the grayling, for even if this dorsal fin were unnoticed, the fish has a mother-of-pearl shimmer to its flanks, though the general impression of the back and dorsal fin when first seen in struggle against hook and line is that you have struck a purple fish.

Appreciation of grayling is a matter of personal taste. On chalk streams they are exterminated as an unwelcome competitor for trout food. In many Continental countries, Austria for example, they are rated higher than trout, perhaps due to that strange bitter-sweet flavour they possess when cooked. For myself, I love them because they are a lucky fish. I may well have taken more specimen grayling than any other species, and many of these were on the dry fly intended for trout on the River Test. A fine specimen would weigh three pounds, and fish over two pounds are exceptional.

In the North of England they are well thought of, though they do not penetrate into the Highlands of Scotland. They prefer clean, fastish rivers without extremes of cold. In spite of continuous warfare they maintain a firm fin-hold on our chalk streams of the south, rivers like the Test, Itchen, Avon and Wylie. I detect today a slightly more tolerant attitude to them among younger water-keepers, a belief, perhaps, that the fly-fishing season might be extended for some into the colder months of later autumn when the grayling are in peak of fighting and eating condition.

Grayling, except when they are rising, may be harder to find in their lies than trout, for though they like fastish rivers, they tend to hang in the streamy, deeper places, especially over gravelly beds and the hollows of weir-pool tails. They are shoaling fish, and when you find one you may expect more in the same place. They usually lie deeper than trout, hugging the bottom from where they have a particularly wide angle of vision above. Their sight seems keener than that of trout, for from this deep position they are able to rise vertically with great speed to take some morsel from the surface. An observer from a bridge may think a fly has passed safely over a grayling, only to watch

The large dorsal fin is a feature of the grayling

it fall victim to this sudden lunge. It frequently amazes me to see the delicacy of the sipping rise from a fish coming so violently from the depths.

Time and time again we have been forced to admit that observation – the basic matter of just watching fish – is essential for understanding how we must proceed.

Suppose you were looking into the grayling pool from the bridge and you saw a floating fly coming downstream over the deep-lying grayling which, at the very last second, shot up to take the fly, what conclusions would you draw? Firstly, you would know that dry-fly is possible even if the grayling is hugging the bottom, for it takes surface fly from this depth. Secondly, you would realise from this sudden, shooting rise that you would have to strike very quickly on seeing the 'take', with none of that slight pause for trout.

Keep watching! The grayling returns to its position, close to the bottom, then shoots up again. Unlike the trout, it doesn't rise higher and higher in the water in the intensity of a hatch of natural fly. This fish can be as keyed on to the hatch as keenly as a trout without varying in any way its place in the pool. Now you see it miss a fly completely, not an unusual event. You see the grayling coming at a hatch of Olives and you know you would catch it on an artificial copy. Then, when the flies come down the stream no longer, the grayling ceases to rise. Suddenly it shoots up to a single sedge.

Dry-fly Approach

We conclude that grayling will rise to a hatch of fly, seemingly with pre-occupation, but with that fixation on the same dun or spinner, typical of a preoccupied trout. Because it lies so deep, reacts so swiftly, the precise shade, size, and shape of the floater is less important, though posture is. The dry fly must float well, have a good stiff hackle and preferably a silicone solution treatment to waterproof it. It must sail downstream erect upon the surface, not floundering along like a waterlogged seed-pod. The dry-fly attack should be based on a similar fly to hatching duns, switching to an attractive pattern between periods of surface activity. For the latter, a killing fly on the Test is Terry's Terror, having a tail of yellow and orange hair and a fine copper tinsel rib on the peacock herl body, with a stiff cock's hackle of Rhode Island red.

As with trout, the evening rise is the propitious time. It explains why grayling are so unpopular on chalk streams. I once took a brace of grayling, each well over 2 lb., during the short period of the dusk hour, until a cold, white mist drifted from the meadows to skill sport that evening. The fish were rising everywhere to the Sherry Spinner, the female imago of the Blue-winged Olive Dun. The population was mixed, brown and rainbow trout with grayling, and the light was so poor as to prevent me from telling one from the other. I selected two steadily rising fish the size of which deceived me into thinking of them as big rainbows. Being a grayling lover, I was delighted, and somewhat piqued when my companion, on seeing them, said 'Bad luck!'

Two other facts emerge when thinking of dry-fly fishing for grayling, firstly that drag doesn't always worry them, nor even the line passing over their heads, and secondly that they will still rise to surface in the quite cold weather of late Autumn, probably to tiny gnats or smuts invisible from a distant bank. A small red- or orange-tagged dry fly will usually tempt them up in these conditions.

Of course grayling can be caught on the upstream nymph and spiders, fished as previously described for trout, yet I prefer to fish downstream with the wet fly, if only because these fish lie deep and are fast enough to seize wet flies sweeping quickly round in the current. No one can really say where downstream fishing starts and upstream begins, and were it not for rules on some chalk streams the difference would be academic. On Border rivers like the Teviot, a tributary of the Tweed, no such rules apply. The term 'downstream' means that the current dictates whether you must cast directly across, even slightly upstream, or angle the flies downstream.

Wet-fly Attack

I can see in my mind's eye a typical run where I caught a big Teviot grayling. I was wading in mid-stream down a tongue of gravel with fast, deeper water on either side, joining below into a deepish pool. As the flies came round in the current, below me, the grayling took hold. I landed him by hand after playing.

In this position I was compelled by physical factors, speed of water, depth and my stance to cast alternately into each bank at a fairly sharp angle downstream. We may discuss upstream or downstream policy, or lay it down in advance, but once in the water the choice will be made for us by the river itself, and the experience dictates how and where the flies must fish. It's that simple, but wet-fly fishing downstream is by no means as easy as described in some books for beginners.

The author lands a grayling by hand. The fish, when played out, is drawn across the author's body while on the surface

Let's start with some basic choices. I prefer a longish rod, say of 10 ft., for these broad rivers of the Border country. I use a light line, usually five or six on the A.F.T.M. scale. It has been written by experts that the floating line is best. Often it is, but on other occasions the slow sinking line, equivalent to a Wet-Cel 1, is better. Why not the sinking-tipped fly line? They don't hang responsively from rod-tip to fly as well as a line made from the same material along its entire length, suitable as they are for many other types of fly work. The old-fashioned ungreased silk lines are ideal for 'hanging a fly in the current'. Now all of this is hard to put into words as once again we meet that mysterious matter of 'being in touch with the fly'. One author recommending the use of floating lines also discussed problems of false bites, of missing fish on a long line and other difficulties caused by the flow, most of which could have been overcome by changing the spool of his reel with another loaded with a slow-sinking line. What it boils down to is this: when grayling are lying deep without inclination to come to the surface, as in cold, overcast conditions of early winter, the fly must be taken down to them, preferably by line weight rather than using the leaded flies, so awkward to cast, so prone to become snagged, so unlikely to work realistically.

It's true that both spider patterns and nymphs will catch fish downstream. Nevertheless my own preference is for small-winged wet flies with light-coloured bodies in summer, such as the Greenwell, and brighter bodies in the colder months. An example of the latter could have a body of orange silk, grouse wing and a snippet of grouse hackle. If spider patterns are to be used downstream it's best to dub in a substantial 'thorax', as in the Tups Indispensable, to force the legs to stand out from the hook shank, freeing them to work with a kick. The choice of flies is vast, and most anglers would fish three.

A good 'summer' team is Greenwell on the point, Rough Olive on the middle, and a small silver fly like a Butcher as top dropper. In winter I use something like my Partridge & Orange, March Brown and Black Spider, for only one of these flies need be bright. The sizes of the summer flies may be small, say 14 or even 16, the smallest fly being lowest on the leader. In colder weather you may go up to size 12.

Downstream wet-fly fishing has an attractive simplicity. You start at the head of a pool or run, casting down and across, letting the fly come onto the dangle, then, moving down another yard or so, you roll out another cast. Every so often you feel a pluck, occasionally a fish is hooked. The current straightens the line nicely for the poor caster. The greatest danger is in the method becoming automatic, in the fisherman losing his concentration.

To lead flies properly through runs, past weed beds, and to fish them at the right speed and depth requires a rare degree of concentration. Running water reflects on the surface the nature of the stream bed over which it flows. At its most elementary, we learn that still waters run deep, that fast stickles are shallow. As we fish on, we should be able to build up a picture of the under-water features of the river by reading its surface shape, its whorls and its knots. We should know, for example, when we are leading the flies into heads of deepening pools, or where obstacles cause little dead-spots in the current, or even back-flows which will reverse the way in which the flies work.

Dry-fly fishing on the
Dorset Stour where grayling
abound

The expert reads these, understands how to cast and work his flies to suit them,
and where fish will lie in relation to them. It's not only a matter of wading
downstream and casting the flies across to let the current do its will. With
grayling, I dare to say the heresy that if this art is mastered the pattern of the
wet fly is relatively unimportant, your faith in it being of greater value than
that of the fish!

My favourite patterns probably don't appear as formal names in the lists
of famous flies. They are basically combinations of body-silks, wings and
hackles to serve the simple philosophy I outlined on fly choice. For those who
have to buy popular patterns by name, here are some renowned for grayling
fishing:

> Wickham's Fancy
> Red Tag
> Orange Tag
> Witch
> Black Gnat
> Orange Bumble
> Waterhen Bloa
> Steel Blue
> Treacle Parkin

11   Memorable Casts

Viscount Grey of Falloden is remembered for watching the lights go out all over Europe in 1914. In fly-fishing he is renowned for describing the progress of the angler through three successive stages. At first he wants to catch as many fish as possible. Then the largest fish are his ambition, but eventually he becomes fascinated by the difficult fish. Difficult fish may exist in all shapes and sizes, but all anglers know what they are.

It might be the two pounder which rises safely below a bush, the branches of which sweep so lovingly against the water that no fly may be inserted between the two. Another trout will lie where a subtle combination of currents will cause a fly to drag so unnaturally that it offers no temptation. Yet another lies close to a sunken log in the corner of the lake, and is so huge that every time a startled angler hooks it the leader is broken summarily. Whatever the cause, these survivors are known to us as 'educated' fish.

After we have graduated to stage three, the memory undergoes a change. From the depths of the fireside chair, the settle in the pub or the stupefying comfort of the bath, it sends up to the surface of consciousness the recollection of perfect casts made in previous years. The biggest fish are forgotten, unless they figured in a tortuous presentation of the fly. The most numerous catches are discarded by the memory as of little value. The challenge is everything.

Reaching this Seventh Heaven was the reason for the first word of the first chapter. If I dredge up these memories it is because they represent our final test, the proof that I'm a fly-fisherman, and by that same token the yardstick by which you can measure your own steps along the right path. If the most, or the biggest fish are more important to you than the interesting ones, then you have some way still to go. Why is it that with fat lakes and chalk streams to fish, I often prefer to return to that scarifyingly difficult stream of my youth? It's because the problems of fly-fishing fill the mind.

So I must take my first memory-draught from that meagre water, and it also takes me back to those days when I felt such excitement on reading Frank Sawyer's nymph-fishing techniques, which proves to me that he is the most significant innovator of fly-fishing ideas since the war, at least as far as chalk-stream trout are concerned.

On this calm summer's evening I was strolling with two friends along the

134

high banks overlooking the stream, more with the intention of interesting them in the unfolding coil of life below us than in serious fishing, for neither of them at that time was an angler. I saw the tiniest of dimpling rises, which I attributed to a dace so quiet and smooth was it. I wasn't nervous at this time, not intending to demonstrate prowess. Besides which I was new to the upstream nymph and unfamiliar with the Pheasant Tail pattern I had tied on.

Slipping into the stream below the place where I had marked the rise I watched the nymph pitch above, sink a few inches and start to drift back to me. The leader pulled down, the surface bulged slightly and I was astonished to find myself tightening into one of our angry little Teise warriors, the scarlet-spotted brownies the river bred in those days. My pleasure came because this was straight out of the book, a classical nymph tactic, and I had just fished enough in Sawyer's way to realise that, compared with my ingrained dry-fly habits, the initiation was damned hard.

Many of my personal one-upmanship stories come from the application of new methods. I remember vividly the sweat of teaching my unwillingly left-hand to cast a short straight line, to open up a new direction of attack to trout which were quite safe from me on the Test. It was a gruelling business because I'm strongly right-handed as well as being fairly slow at acquiring physical skills, though once mastered they stick. I had taken my first trout with a left-handed cast, and a week later I came to a different beat.

This beat was a place of great contrast. The river divided like two trouser-legs branching away from a waist. The left leg was shallow, wide, open and fast. The right branch was deep, sluggish and towards the limit it curled through a murderously tangled spinney in such a way that normal right-handed casts had to be trapped behind in the undergrowth. My hope was that I could now execute a left-handed side-cast above the curving stream. The exposed parts of the river were being scoured by an overbearing wind. Under the trees it was quiet, the sunlight dappled the water and the noise of the wind was shut out.

I knelt down to watch the deepish tail of a pool where it licked under trailing willows. This was the day of the Grannom, an early-season sedge which delights in the daylight hours, unlike most of its dusk-loving family. Sure enough one of these brownish flies came bouncing along until it coincided with a darkish shape looming up from the shadow of the pool, and in a twinkling it was gone into the depths with the rainbow. The day was stretching before me, the wind shouting round the corners of the wood was telling me to hide myself in this quiet corner, and for these reasons I had all the time to prepare the attack with cool nerves.

I eased myself back to the lip of the bank, and took a hard look at the casting problem. At once I grasped the advantage that those pedantic left-handed casting sessions now gave me. The leader would fall in a delightful shepherd's crook, keeping nylon away from the fish and allowing the fly to ride over the trout, unpreceded by line or leader. The low cast, close to the surface, would neutralise shadow and flash. And so it came to pass that I caught four thumping rainbows there, in the silent tunnel under the trees. The fifth, my last permissible trout, came unstuck only because my unaccustomed left-arm muscles were too weak to set the hook. And then the

Grannom no longer came down. Instead, upstream, some oaf shook out an eel trap, the muddied commotion from which put paid to that pool for that day. In the sun-bleached, wind-swept open water, my more powerful right arm and long-thrown line reaped no harvest at all.

A Cast at Two Lakes

I now remember the last trout I caught on a split cane rod. The rod was a Fario Club, given to me in Paris by Jacques Michel, then sales manager of the firm of Pezon & Michel. This rod was surely one of the most expensive in the world, a fly fisherman's Stradivarius. It was light, yet powerful, with a strange action enabling it to push out twenty yards of a light, size 5 fly line. The place was Two Lakes, the first and greatest of the small commercial still-water fisheries, lying between the Rivers Test and Itchen. These lakes, by then swollen to six from the original two, were cradled in woodland, and they were stocked with trout of enormous girth.

The time was May, the month of the Sepia Dun, which is a smallish, dark-brown member of the Ephemeridae. These flies were hatching in front of me, too far in front, and a trout had been cruising in a lazy circle just beyond my best range. His passage was marked by snorty little whirlpools as he chopped up the Sepia Duns as they broke surface to hatch. After an hour or so this fish stayed consistently beyond range and I was debating whether or not to move to fresh hunting grounds when he made a sudden foray of about a yard towards me. I whipped up the little cane rod, gave the line a good double-haul and shot for all my worth.

I admit to a streak of luck, for the fly pitched virtually on his snout and he gulped it down in the fastest cast-rise-strike sequence I've yet made. That French lightweight made short shrift of his lunges for open water and three pounds of thrashing brownie were bundled into the net. The fly was a Sepia Dun with the hackles clipped to make a short supporting collar to hold the fly in the surface film.

The rod had a sad history after that brief hour of glory. The following week, preparing to leave early for Two Lakes, I left the rod propped against my motor-bike in the empty street. My wife called me back to have a quick look at our young son who had just woken with a slight fever. We decided to 'wait and see', but in that short wait, the rod was stolen and the street still empty on my return to the machine.

The three rainbows, each over six pounds, which I may boast of, were by no means memorable fish. I fear they were all introduced into the lakes I fished not many days before I caught them. Their fight was unexceptional. Give me a spritely three-pounder any day for courage and dash.

Fish which remain vividly in the memory are sometimes those taken when, according to angling lore, conditions were impossible. Sometimes there's more than a grain of truth in these myths. Generally dry-fly fishing does cease when the first cold mists drift from the water-meadows. Either they chill the surface too rapidly, or, more likely, they destroy visibility.

Perhaps the exceptions prove the rule, for I was prepared once to take down my rod during an evening rise on the Test. It was a warm July, but the ghostly wraiths started to seep from the long grass. I shrugged my shoulders in disgust, staring moodily up the rapidly vanishing river, then, from below the vapour, I heard plot after plop. Some spinners were still falling onto the water, and being part of the surface film the fish could still see them. Mist is very uneven on a river; it leaves some areas of water clear, and I was able to put a Red Spinner to a trout rising between a trailing branch and the bank. It took boldly enough and by the time I'd landed it my clothing was damp from the clamminess in the air.

Apart from old wives' tales, there are also other 'weather maxims'. These have the effect of either excusing failure or destroying confidence. We already know the conditions under which fish *may* refuse to feed, and they are confined

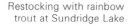

Restocking with rainbow trout at Sundridge Lake

to extremes of heat and cold, lack of oxygen in the water, and when vision is impeded, as in really turbid water. Yet I have been told that salmon will never take a fly when the sky is red, or the wind is making arrow-shaped ruffles on the water, which is mostly nonsense.

The effect of all these preconceived obstacles is to block the mind to tactical choice of fishing method, based on observation. And whereas it's comfortable to have excuses off the shelf, anglers who fall into this erroneous way of thinking eventually wind up by reeling from catch-phrase to catch-phrase when all they need to do is think through the problems. After all, we can't expect instant success, and few experts in game fishing hope to base their reputations on tremendous catches. The expert is aiming at some consistency in his fishing, winkling out his opponents on good days and bad. If a reservoir angler could guarantee two or three fish on each outing he would settle for this over a season, rather than a huge slaughter of innocent trout in early April, followed by doldrums in the dog-days of summer.

Let's examine the other side of the coin: it's true today that thanks to intensive put-and-take trout stocking there are times when trout are too easy to catch. When first I turned to the smaller lake fisheries I even deceived myself for a while that I was the greatest angler ever, sometimes catching rainbows of several pounds with consecutive casts. I knew little then of fishery management, believing in my innocence that these fish were as hard to deceive as the little wildies I fished for when young. When I, too, was forced to adopt a similar stocking policy for my own fishery I became so cynical for a year or two that I felt self-disgust when catching these stew-bred idiots. For some time I could hardly bear to fish for them.

One of the things we have lost from the past is the old spirit of sportsmanship towards the opponent. The deep-freeze may well have a lot to answer for! I reached a personal balance in returning safely to the water most of the fish I hooked, confident that I had probably made it more difficult to catch them in future. I also abandoned the lure on small lakes, even where rules permit them, and concentrated more and more on imitative fishing. Finally, I began to learn the areas dominated by isolated large trout, which I would wait for, watching to see when they started to feed. This restored an interest in what otherwise could have been an artificial situation.

Specimen Hunting

An example of this once occurred when I had marked down four large rainbows in Sundridge lake, each of which had been in the fishery for long enough to become acclimatised and as wild and wary as farm-rainbows ever grow. Each of these fish seemed to be well over six pounds, and dominated an area from which it drove smaller rivals.

I arrived at dawn while the mists were still seeping from the bankside grass and drifting across the lakes. Everything was quiet, promising a hot, bright day when only these first few hours offer any hope. Being undisturbed during the night, the large fish could be expected to move from their deep holes in search of food before the first noisy paddle strokes broke over their heads. The first fish lay immediately in front of the fishing hut where a small declivity

in the lake floor offered shelter. As I tackled up I saw him heave up the surface of the water as he moved onto a nymph or small fish. Although I watched for another twenty minutes, he came not again. A few casts in the area produced no response.

I then quietly paddled a boat towards the deep hole where a half-sunken log protrudes from the bank. A monstrous brown trout lived here, but there was no sign at all of activity, the water being dark and quiet in the shadow. I knew of another big fish occupying an area of open water, and as I approached him up he went into the air in a great fountain of spray. This isn't a good sign. Such fish are usually moving far and fast, possibly from a deep weed-bed from which they flush nymphs or small fish which they pursue to the surface. Several casts again produced no response, nor did this fish leap again.

The ideal situation is to find a large trout gently rolling over nymphs below the surface. The next quarry rules a small bay behind an island. It was his habit to drive his food against a shelving bank where he trapped it. I moored the punt above this place, while behind me the sun was growing hotter as it burned off the Wealden mists. My patience was rewarded as I saw the big rainbow turning onto a nymph about a foot below the surface, twelve yards in front of me. He was very red, a sure sign of an old inhabitant. I cast an Invicta wet fly in his path, and as I drew it gently towards an interception point the line tightened and he was well hooked, a fine specimen of 6 lb. 2 oz., the only fish I've bothered to keep in replica form as a souvenir of Sundridge. This is typical of the summer visits I made to the lakes, often seeing no one, no living creature apart from solitary herons, or once a playful pair of otters bouncing along the bank. I used to leave for breakfast as the first of the regular anglers was arriving. The hefty fish from the first hole was caught a few months later, weighing 8 lb. 2 oz.

While we may all find ways to restore the balance of intensively stocked fisheries in favour of sportsmanship, it remains true that while we must accept the economic necessities for them we haven't come to terms with the changing values they impose. For all their faults, their snobbery and occasional dogmas, the previous generations of fly-fishermen would have been disgusted with modern 'instant trout', and particularly with the early season or stockfish slaughter. Its only virtue is to encourage the novice. Its greatest danger lies in persuading management to adopt policies to satiate the 'deep-freeze' demand. If the time ever comes when the commercial fisheries are in the hands of non-angling accountants the 'dude fishery' will become respectable.

As it is, one of the greatest problems we have to solve is the decline of sporting standards in fly-fishing. In still-water and chalk-stream we need to devise a code which on the one hand gives stock trout a chance to acclimatise themselves to a wild environment, and on the other encourages anglers to respect the concept of fish being the reward for skill, not merely a reward for money invested in permits. I must confess to being pessimistic, for I'm unable to persuade even those I know quite well that trout-lust is gaining the upper hand, and that the pinnacle of pleasure on still-water at any rate should not be to drag a lure through a host of recently stocked rainbows.

There are many remedies. One of the best is to open rainbow fisheries on the first of May, having the bulk of stockfish introduced in March or earlier, gaining time to allow them to change from hand-feeding to the search for natural food. Most rainbows are in poor shape in April, but an extension of the season to the end of October would find still-water rainbows in first-class condition.

Returning to the individual angler, I once gave an instructional talk to a club, much along the lines of this book, in discussing the tackle, the techniques and the way in which you absorb information from the environment. A questioner asked me, 'Once you are reasonably proficient at a practical level, what else should you do to improve?'

The answer is strange. You should learn to relax. I find this extraordinarily difficult, being by nature rather tense, and there's no more bizarre contradiction than the command 'try to relax!', for the act of concentration is enough to tense up those of us untrained in Yoga. Concentration and relaxation are opposites. This is never more true than in casting a dry fly or nymph to a fish, the rise of which one sometimes anticipates with a lightning reflex that pulls the hook straight out of its mouth.

The relaxation is a by-product of my advice to watch fish. The first temptation on finding a rising trout or restless salmon is to put the fly to it while you still sense its mood of excitement. In hurrying, being over-tense, you can easily mess up the cast or strike. If you force yourself to watch, not only do the nerves subside but you may well see some improved way to present the fly as against your earlier automatic reaction to be at the fish. Then, when you've schooled yourself, you can make the cast, strike the fish at the critical time, and play it out in a way you have had time to plan, having noticed any snags or obstacles to which the fish could run. Then you have in reality achieved the essence of relaxed concentration.

One still-water victory clings to my mind since it involved a stalk of several hundred yards. I came to Sundridge lake on a sultry afternoon with little chance of a fish before dusk. Having put together my rod I idly scanned the lake through binoculars when, in a far bay, where the water was shallow, I saw a ring breaking the surface, then another. I took a punt to the top of the lake to watch the activity at close range. I saw a rainbow of about two pounds moving in a circle, in maybe less than two feet of water and feeding on small gnats hatching there.

I made a wide detour to come to the head of the bay, beyond the fish, while I thought out my campaign. The cast would need to be long, yet gentle because there was absolutely no breeze to ruffle the water. I chose a dry Grey Duster, being the best copy I know of the myriads of drab gnats that frequently populate the surfaces of lakes in summer. I was sure I'd reached my position without alarming the quarry. I let down the anchor as if it were nitro-glycerine. Then I watched some more. The trout continued to feed on its circular beat, undisturbed by my approach.

The first cast alighted slightly to the right, but I guessed immediately that it was no good. The trout wasn't scared, it just didn't believe that my fly was edible. And perhaps I never would have cadged him to take it had not a slight movement of air whipped over the water, bringing up a short, bright ripple. Seeing the fish move below the broken surface, I cast the dry fly again. It fell in front of his nose, and was snaffled without hesitation.

For the newcomer to fly-fishing, every trout will be a landmark at first. He reads with amazement the inference that he will reach a stage when he no longer recalls his daily catches, and that only exceptional or difficult fish will be remembered. It is true, and as he graduates to the stage of taking a few hundred fish each year, only a week or two has to pass to wipe the slate clear of average fish caught on average days. When you find that happening you'll know you've reached maturity as a fly-fisherman!

Appendix: The Flies

The following is a list of the chief flies used by the author for the various techniques described in this book. The details of the dressings are included for those who wish to delve deeper into the art of fly tying.

River Dry Flies

Large Dark Olive (Early Season Fly)
- Hook   – size 12
- Tail   – blue dun cock
- Body   – blue mole's fur mixed with a pinch of dark olive seal's fur
- Rib   – gold wire
- Hackle – A few turns of blue dun cock mixed with dark olive

March Brown for Fast Water (Early Season Fly)
- Hook   – size 12
- Tail   – fibres from a brown partridge flank feather
- Body   – brown fur from a hare's ear
- Rib   – gold wire
- Hackle – brown partridge flank feather in front of two stiff white cock's hackles
  This fly is intended to show up well, and to float on fast, broken water

Iron Blue Dun (Early Season)
- Hook   – 14 to 16
- Tail   – blue dun cock
- Body   – blue mole's fur spun onto red silk which also makes a small tag
- Hackle – dark blue dun cock

Rough Olive (Summer)
- Hook size – 12 – 14
- Tail   – olive cock
- Body   – medium olive seal's fur
- Rib   – gold wire
- Hackle   – medium olive cock

Pale Olive (Summer)

Hook size – 14 – 16
Tail	– light olive cock
Body	– pale olive seal's fur
Rib	– gold wire
Hackle	– pale olive cock

Red Spinner (Summer)

Hook size   – 14
Tail	– white cock
Body	– red floss silk
Rib	– fine flat gold tinsel
Hackle	– red game cock
Wings (optional)	– grey starling, upright

Green Champion Mayfly

Hook	– 8 to 12 long shank
Tail	– three cock pheasant tail fibres
Body	– apple green floss silk
Rib	– black button thread
Hackle	– short badger cock palmered down body, and another wound at throat
Wings	– two brown partridge flank feathers, dyed green and tied forward with little splay

Spent Gnat (Spinner)

Hook	– as above
Tail	– three cock pheasant tail fibres
Body	– white floss silk
Rib	– black button thread
Hackle	– badger, at throat only, short and lightly wound
Wings	– two pairs of black cock hackle points tied 'spent' on either side of the hook

Sedge (Summer)

Hook	– size 12 to 14
Body	– brown hare's ear
Rib	– gold wire
Hackles	– 1. red game cock palmered
	2. red game at throat
Wings	– brown hen wing quill feather, rolled and tied flat

Black Gnat (all seaon fly)

Hook	– 12 to 16
Body	– black floss silk
Hackle	– black cock

The above ten flies are a selection which will serve on any river in Britain throughout the season. They are arranged in seasonal order, except for the Mayflies which have their special season at the end of May to the beginning of June.

Upstream Spiders

Black Spider
   Body   – brown silk
   Hackle – two turns of hackle from a starling's wing or body

Red Spider
   Body   – red silk, gold wire rib is optional
   Hackle – two turns brown hen

Greenwell Spider
   Body   – yellow silk, gold wire rib
   Hackle – Greenwell or light brown hen, two turns

Tups Spider
   Body   – yellow silk with a dubbing of pink tup's wool for the thorax
   Hackle – honey hen, two turns

Hares' Ear Spider
   Body   – hares ear fur spun lightly on yellow silk, with gold wire rib
   Hackle – brown partridge flank feather, two turns

Iron Blue Spider
   Body   – purple silk with light dubbing of mole's fur
   Hackle – dark blue dun hen, two turns

The above patterns are for upstream wet-fly fishing, the size of hook to be determined by season. The darker patterns and the March Brown Spider suit the early and late seasons. They are intended to suit any rivers in Britain and Ireland.

Upstream Nymphs

Iron Blue
   Tail   – tips of three strands of smokey-blue heron herl . . . .
   Body   – which are then wound up two thirds of the shank to form the abdomen, ribbed with fine copper wire
   Thorax   – a knob of blue mole's fur dubbed to the silk and wound in front of the abdomen
   Wing cases – three or four strands of the same heron herl tied in behind the thorax and brought over it . . .
   Legs   – to be divided on top of the hook shank into equal parts, separated on either side of the hook by figure-of-eight turns of thread, clipped short.

The following patterns follow this same structure

Pheasant Tail
Body & Tail	– reddish strands of fibre from a cock pheasant's tail
Rib	– copper wire
Thorax	– strands of cock pheasant tail twisted together
Wing Case & Legs	– six strands of the same over the thorax and clipped short

Grey Goose Nymph
This follows the same structure using the grey herl from a goose wing and copper wire rib

March Brown Nymph
The same structure again, but using a brown herl from a cinnamon turkey tail feather and gold wire rib.

Olive Nymph
As above using dyed olive swan herl and a gold rib

These five nymphs will serve all stream fishing needs, while three of them, the Olive, Pheasant Tail and Grey Goose nymphs have caught many fish on still water. They are 'true' nymphs, that is imitations of this stage of Ephemeridae.

Still-water Flies

Flies for still-water fishing break down into several categories. Some specialists carry huge cases containing thousands of flies, but at a strictly practical level this is hardly necessary. I list here reliable patterns in the different categories with the note that I rarely carry more.

Lures

Church Fry
Hook	– sizes 6 & 8 long shank
Body	– first two thirds of orange floss silk with fine flat gold rib. Last third of magenta fluorescent silk or wool
Hackle	– a few fibres of magenta cock hackle
Wing	– grey squirrel tail

White Minnow
Hook	– size 6 or 8 long shank
Tail	– a bunch of marabou fibres, or any whitish hackle wound round hook
Body	– white fluorescent wool, shaped like the body of a small fish, ribbed with silver tinsel
Hackle	– short orange cock hackles, tied as a beard
Wing	– a strip of barred teal
Head	– built up with black tying silk, covered with several layers of varnish and with a small white dot painted on either side to simulate eyes

Black Minnow
Hook	– size 6 or 8 long shank
Body	– black wool or floss silk for the first two thirds, scarlet fluorescent wool for the last third, and silver oval tinsel over both.

Hackle – beard hackle of scarlet cock
Wing   – dyed black goat's hair
Head   – built up with tying silk, several layers of varnish and a coat of silver paint over this. Painted eyes optional

Black-nosed Dace
Hook   – size 6 or 8 long shank
Tail   – two strands of scarlet fluorescent wool
Body   – flat silver tinsel or lurex ribbed with fine silver oval tinsel
Wing   – grey squirrel
Head   – built up with black tying thread, varnished

Silver Fry
Body   – silver tinsel, ribbed silver wire
Wing   – green over orange pairs of cock hackles, tied streamer fashion
Hackles– green and orange hackles wound together as a collar in front of wing

Note – this fly is also tied with a gold body on any size of hook, long in the shank and is effective in waters containing perch fry.

There are many other lures. I have listed those of my own adaptation and not repeated here the standard patterns, which have proved successful. They are the family of Muddler Minnows (brown, white, orange, yellow, black) the various Polystickles and Sinfoil Fry, the Sweeney Todd, Breathalyser, Baby Doll, Jersey Herd and so forth, which are all proved killers.

The patterns I have recommended typify both schools of lure, the one with a hairwing, the other streamer-style with two pairs of cock hackles for wings, set on top of the hook, side by side.

I have also given dressings for patterns of mine which serve two purposes, that of general attractor for the 'random feeding' behaviour, described earlier, as well as for fish feeding with preoccupation on gatherings of small fish.

The Nymphs

The following patterns are loosely called nymphs, in the sense that they are closer representations of still water fauna than general wet flies.

Buzzer Pupae
The bodies are of various colours to suit the water, orange, green, black, brown, olive, claret, red. The body material starts round hook-bend.
Hook sizes – 8 to 18
Body   – fluorescent floss to choice, ribbed with fine silver tinsel, then covered in a layer or two of clear varnish or liquid plastic
Thorax – matching fluorescent wool, teased out and dubbed onto the silk, then wound in a small knob in front of the abdomen
Head   – two or three turns of peacock herl with a doubled length of white floss silk tied on top of the hook, pointing forwards to copy breathing tubes

Footballer

Hook	– as above
Body	– alternate bands of black and white horsehair wound side by side from well round hook bend, to form abdomen
Thorax	– moles fur dubbed in as a small knob
Head	– peacock herl

Caddis Case (sedge larva)

Hood	– size 10 or 12 long shank
Body	– brown or olive ostrich herl
Back	– strip of matching nylon raffia along top of the body, varnished
Head	– matching cock hackle, clipped short

Amber Nymph (Sedge pupa)

Hood	– sizes 8 to 14
Body	– first two thirds amber seal's fur, second part of dark brown or claret seal's fur
Back	– a strip of brown nylon raffia, varnished
Hackle	– a tuft of brown cock tied as a beard

Corixa (Water Boatman)

Hook	– sizes 8 to 14
Tag	– oval silver tinsel
Body	– light brown fur from a hare's mask, ribbed with silver. The body should be weighted with 5 amp fuse wire if fished on a floating line
Back	– brown nylon raffia, varnished
Paddles	– four cock pheasant tail fibres, divided on either side of the hook, and left about $\frac{1}{4}''$ long, varnished.

The lake and pond olives are virtually the same nymph patterns as the Medium Olive Nymph for stream fishing. Although the Pheasant Tail is suitable for the nymph of the dark brown Sepia Dun, a special nymph can be made in the same style, simply using a dark-brown swan herl.

The above represent the chief nymph patterns to succeed on virtually any water, but even so, they are a fraction of the artificials which can be made from descriptions in specialised books, and Damsel Nymphs, Hoglouse, Shrimp, and many others can be added in profusion, according to local conditions.

Being too numerous to mention here, I recommend the specialised books for further study in the still-water chapter, and I content myself with the observation that the patterns given above should account for at least 75% of trout feeding on still-water.

Three patterns for fishing the bottom in deep water –

Hoglouse

Hook size	– 10, 12
Legs	– grey partridge hackle wound at tail-end of hook, so that fibres trail to rear
Body	– hare's body fur, ribbed with silver oval tinsel

Fresh Water Shrimp

Hook	– size 10 – 12
Body	– pale-olive seal's fur, dubbed on to make a hump-backed shape
Rib	– flat gold tinsel

Legs – a small bunch of pale-olive hen hackle fibres tied as a beard hackle

Back – a strip of pale-olive raffine, varnished, tied flat along the top of the body

Black & Peacock Spider (snail, beetle etc.)

Hook – 6 to 14

Body – twisted bunch of bronze peacock herl over an underbody of black floss silk, bug-shaped.

Hackle – two turns only of long black hen

Still-water Dry Flies

Dry Buzzers

Hook – sizes 12–16

Body – coloured silk to choice (green, black, orange red etc.) with clear nylon over

Thorax – teased out fluorescent wool dubbed on immediately behind hackle and wings

Wings – two white hackle points, sloping backwards

Hackle – white or badger cock

Brown Sedge

Hook – sizes 10 to 14, or large 6 & 8 for Murragh Fly.

Body – brown hare's ear fur, ribbed gold wire

Hackle – 1. Red game cock palmered down body
2. Ditto at throat only

Wings – brown hen wing quill, tied flat

White Moth

Hook – large 6 down to 14

Body – white fluorescent wool, tied fat, ribbed flat silver tinsel

Wing – white goose, tied flat

Hackle – two white cock hackles at throat only

Brown Moth (Hoolet)

Hook – sizes 6 & 8

Body – twisted bronze peacock herls over a sliver of cork

Wing – brown owl tied flat

Hackle – two red game cock hackles wound at throat only.

Crane Fly (Daddy Longlegs)

Hook – 8 to 12 long shank, normal shank for detached body.

Body – brown plastic detached body on smaller hook, or cinnamon turkey herl with gold ribbed on long hook

Legs – six strands of ginger horsehair, knotted in middle, and divided on either side of hook

Hackle – two light brown cock hackles, points being tied down flat on either side of hook to form the wings

I use many standard flies. The patterns given above are 'specials'. Such patterns as the Invicta, for sedge hatches, Grey Duster for caenis, Olives, Terrestial flies like ants, can all be found in text-books on fly tying.

Notes on Salmon Flies

Flies used by myself are also standard patterns, but the fully dressed patterns have a slim wing, made by reducing the number of strands of feather in the built wings.

Hair-wing flies have light bunches of hair, tied low. Patterns I recommend are:

Thunder & Lightning in all four styles, that is fully dressed, low-water, tube-fly and hair wings. This is probably the most killing salmon fly in use today in any part of the world.

For bright sunlight, the Silver Blue, fully dressed or low-water is recommended, and for coloured water, the hair-wing Green Highlander.

For sea trout fishing at night, the Teal Blue & Silver is recommended on moonlit rivers, the Connemara Black when very dark with Invictas being successful at dusk. The author often ties these flies on long shanked hooks, and believes that if these flies prove unacceptable, then no other pattern is likely to work.

On very fast waters, Spey patterns like the Lady Caroline and Grey Heron are recommended for salmon, as their long-flowing hackles work well in the current. The dressings for these are in the comprehensive manuals on fly tying by authorities like John Veniard.

Bibliography

BATES, JOSEPH R.: *Atlantic Salmon Flies & Fishing* (Stackpole, 1971)
BUCKNALL, GEOFFREY: *Fly Fishing Tactics on Still Water* (Muller, 1974)
BUCKNALL, GEOFFREY: *Fly Fishing Tactics on Rivers* (Muller, 1968)
BUCKNALL, GEOFFREY: *Fly Tying for Beginners* (Benn, 1972)
CALVER, JIM: *Bank Fishing for Reservoir Trout* (A. & C. Black, 1972)
GODDARD, JOHN: *Trout Fly Recognition* (A. & C. Black, 1972)
GODDARD, JOHN: *Trout Flies of Still Water* (A. & C. Black, 1971)
IVENS, T. C.: *Still Water Fly Fishing* (Deutsch, 1970)
KITE, OLIVER: *Nymph Fishing in Practice* (Barrie & Jenkins, 1971)
OGLESBY, ARTHUR: *Salmon* (MacDonald, 1971)
RYGHNI, R.: Grayling (MacDonald, 1971)
SAWYER, FRANK: *The Nymph & the Trout* (A. & C. Black, 1970)
STEWART. W. C.: *The Practical Angler* (A. & C. Black, 1961)
SKUES, G. E. M.: *The Way of the Trout with a Fly* (A. & C. Black, 1970)
VENIARD, John: *Fly Dressers' Guide:* (A. & C. Black, 1972)
VENIARD, JOHN: *Reservoir & Lake Flies* (A. & C. Black, 1970)
WILLIAMS, A. COURTNEY: *A Dictionary of Trout Flies* (A. & C. Black, 1973)

Index